EXECUTIVE SUMMARY

INTRODUCTION

The Office of the Inspector General (OIG) conducted this review to assess how the Department of Justice's (Department) four law enforcement components respond to sexual misconduct and harassment allegations made against their employees. This review examined the nature, frequency, reporting, investigation, and adjudication of such allegations in the Bureau of Alcohol, Tobacco, Firearms and Explosives (ATF); the Drug Enforcement Administration (DEA); the Federal Bureau of Investigation (FBI); and the United States Marshals Service (USMS).

Issues That Arose During the Review

The OIG's ability to conduct this review was significantly impacted and delayed by the repeated difficulties we had in obtaining relevant information from both the FBI and DEA as we were initiating this review in mid-2013.[1] Initially, the FBI and DEA refused to provide the OIG with unredacted information that was responsive to our requests, citing the *Privacy Act of 1974* and concerns for victims and witnesses as the reasons for the extensive redactions, despite the fact that the OIG is authorized under the Inspector General Act to receive such information.[2]

After months of protracted discussions with management at both agencies, the DEA and FBI provided the information without extensive redactions; but we found that the information was still incomplete. Ultimately, based on a review of information in the OIG Investigations Division databases, we determined that a material number of allegations from both DEA and FBI were not included in the original responses to our request for the information.

---

[1] Both the ATF and the USMS provided the OIG with full, complete, and timely access to our requests.

[2] *See generally Privacy Act of 1974*, Pub. L. 93–579, 88 Stat. 1896, 5 U.S.C. § 552a, which governs the collection, maintenance, use, and dissemination of personally identifiable information about individuals maintained in systems of records by federal agencies, and the Inspector General Act of 1978, § 6(a)(1) (authorizing OIGs "to have access to all records, reports, ... documents, papers, ... or other material available to the [agency] which relate to programs and operations with respect to which that Inspector General has responsibilities under this Act"). Because the OIG is an agency within the Department, and handles information it receives consistent with the requirements of the *Privacy Act,* the FBI and the DEA's failure to provide the information to the OIG at the outset was unwarranted.

We were also concerned by an apparent decision by DEA to withhold information regarding a particular open misconduct case. The OIG was not given access to this case file information until several months after our request, and only after the misconduct case was closed. Once we became aware of the information, we interviewed DEA employees who said that they were given the impression that they were not to discuss this case with the OIG while the case remained open. The OIG was entitled to receive all such information from the outset, and the failure to provide it unnecessarily delayed our work.

Therefore, we cannot be completely confident that the FBI and DEA provided us with all information relevant to this review. As a result, our report reflects the findings and conclusions we reached based on the information made available to us.

RESULTS IN BRIEF

Although we found there were relatively few reported allegations of sexual harassment and sexual misconduct in the Department's law enforcement components for fiscal years 2009 through 2012, our review of the handling of these allegations revealed some significant systemic issues with the components' processes that we believe require prompt corrective action.[3]

Coordination between internal affairs offices and security personnel. At ATF, DEA, and USMS, there was a lack of coordination between the internal affairs offices that receive sexual misconduct allegations and the offices responsible for ensuring that employees meet the requirements to hold security clearances. In most cases where employees were alleged to have engaged in high-risk sexual behavior, security personnel were not informed about these incidents until long after they occurred or were never informed, even though such behavior presents possible significant security risks.[4] By contrast, at the FBI, the

---

[3] We discuss our findings in the *Executive Summary* in the order of importance. However, the *Results of the Review* follow the disciplinary process: reporting, security, investigation, and adjudication.

[4] "High-risk sexual behavior" is defined in *Adjudicative Guidelines for Determining Eligibility for Access to Classified Information,* as conduct that involves "a criminal offense, indicates a personality or emotional disorder, reflects lack of judgment or discretion, or may subject an individual to undue influence or coercion, exploitation, or duress or raise questions about an individual's reliability, trustworthiness and ability to protect classified information." *See* generally, Memorandum from Stephen J. Hadley, White House Assistant to the President for National Security Affairs, *Adjudicative Guidelines for Determining Eligibility for Access to Classified Information*, December 29, 2005.

Internal Investigations Section alerts the Security Division to any misconduct allegations it receives so that a determination can be made as to whether an allegation raises security risks for the FBI or raises concerns about the employee's continued eligibility to hold a security clearance.

Reporting misconduct allegations to component headquarters. ATF and the USMS have clear policies requiring supervisors to report misconduct allegations, including alleged sexual misconduct and sexual harassment, to their headquarters internal affairs offices. However, we found that supervisors sometimes failed to report these allegations, even when the subject was alleged to have committed similar misconduct in the past. We found that the sexual misconduct and sexual harassment reporting policies at the DEA did not clearly delineate what should be reported to headquarters and what should be treated as a local management or performance-related issue. As a result, DEA supervisors exercised discretion in deciding what to report, even when their respective offense tables characterized sexual misconduct and sexual harassment as prohibited behavior. We also found that FBI sexual misconduct reporting policies did not clearly delineate what should be reported to headquarters and what should be treated as a local management or performance-related issue. However, the FBI does have a clear requirement for employees to report all allegations of sexual harassment. In all four components, some allegations were not reported by headquarters to the OIG when they first occurred.

The investigative process. ATF, DEA, and FBI have criteria regarding the opening at headquarters of investigations into allegations of sexual misconduct and sexual harassment. Although ATF generally followed its established criteria, we found instances in which the FBI failed to follow its criteria and instances where DEA failed to fully investigate allegations. The USMS does not have established criteria, but generally seemed to make appropriate determinations about when to initiate an investigation in such matters.

The adjudication process. The ATF offense table does not contain specific offense categories to address sexual misconduct and sexual harassment. The DEA, FBI, and USMS have offense tables that contain specific categories for such allegations and provide guidance on the appropriate range of penalties that could be imposed. We found that the DEA and USMS offense tables do not provide adequate explanations of the types of behaviors that warrant possible disciplinary action. In some instances, these components applied general offense categories to misconduct more appropriately addressed by the specific sexual misconduct and sexual harassment offense categories in their offense tables.

Component offense tables do not always contain language adequate to address the solicitation of prostitutes in jurisdictions where the conduct is legal or tolerated. We found that the ATF, DEA, and USMS offense tables do not contain specific language to address the solicitation of prostitutes abroad, even where the conduct is legal or tolerated. Although the FBI offense table contains such a category, we found instances where general offense categories were applied instead of the specific category. Employees in ATF, DEA, and USMS may not receive adequate notice that this conduct is prohibited or of the range of penalties that could be imposed for it.

All of the components have weaknesses in detecting sexually explicit text messages and images. For all components, we were unable to determine the actual number of instances involving the transmission of sexually explicit text messages and images because the components do not have adequate technology to enable them to detect this type of misconduct. Although the FBI archives and proactively monitors its employees' text messages, there are limitations to its ability to use this information, and misconduct investigators at ATF, DEA, and USMS cannot easily obtain such text message evidence. These issues may hamper the components' ability to use this type of evidence in misconduct investigations, to fully satisfy their discovery obligations, and to deter misconduct.

RECOMMENDATIONS

We make eight recommendations in this report to improve the law enforcement components' disciplinary and security processes relating to allegations of sexual misconduct and harassment.

TABLE OF CONTENTS

INTRODUCTION

The Department of Justice's (Department) law enforcement components are charged with investigating violations of federal law. Given the nature of their work, federal law enforcement employees are held to the highest standards of conduct and must be accountable for their actions both on- and off-duty.

When employees of law enforcement components commit sexual misconduct or sexual harassment, or engage in criminal activity related to prostitution or the exploitation of children, it affects the component's reputation, undermines its credibility, and potentially compromises the government's efforts in prosecutions. Sexual misconduct and sexual harassment in the workplace also affect employee morale and hamper employees' ability to have and maintain effective working relationships. When sexual misconduct involves a criminal element, witness, confidential source, informant, or foreign national, it may also affect the security of the components' operations.

In the past 3 years, there have been allegations of sexual misconduct involving law enforcement agents from a Department component, as well as from another federal law enforcement agency, that have received international media attention. In the wake of our review of the alleged sexual misconduct of several DEA Special Agents in Cartagena, Colombia, the Office of the Inspector General (OIG) initiated this review to assess the nature, frequency, reporting, investigation, and adjudication of allegations of sexual misconduct (including the transmission of sexually explicit texts and images) and sexual harassment in the four Department law enforcement components: the Bureau of Alcohol, Tobacco, Firearms and Explosives (ATF); the Drug Enforcement Administration (DEA); the Federal Bureau of Investigation (FBI); and the United States Marshals Service (USMS).[5]

---

[5] Since disciplinary systems play a significant role in ensuring the efficiency of government services and the fair and equitable treatment of covered employees, the OIG previously performed six reviews assessing the disciplinary systems of the law enforcement components and the Executive Office for United States Attorneys, including the Review of the USAO's and EOUSA's Disciplinary Process, I-2014-001, February 2014; the Federal Bureau of Investigation's Disciplinary System, I-2009-002, May 2009; Review of the Bureau of Alcohol, Tobacco, Firearms and Explosives' Disciplinary System, I-2005-009, September 2005; Review of the Federal Bureau of Prisons' Disciplinary System, I-2004-008, September 2004; Review of the Drug Enforcement Administration's Disciplinary System, I-2004-002, January 2004; and Review of the United States Marshals Service Discipline Process, I-2001-011, September 2001.

Sexual Misconduct and Harassment Defined

For purposes of this review, we utilized the FBI's definition of "sexual misconduct" as "engaging in sexual, intimate, or romantic activity in an inappropriate location (such as government spaces, government vehicles), or while on duty," and also included the following additional separate offense categories[6]:

- Rape;
- Sexual Assault;
- Child Pornography;
- Solicitation of Prostitutes;
- Improper Sexual Association with Confidential Sources, Witnesses, Informants, and Criminal Elements;
- Inappropriate Relationships;
- Misuse of Government Property (Vehicle or Office Space) for Sexual Purposes;
- Misuse of Position to Coerce a Sexual Encounter or Relationship; and
- Sexting (transmission of sexually explicit text, e-mail messages, and images with government equipment).

We used the Equal Employment Opportunity Commission's (EEOC) "Guidelines on Discrimination Because of Sex" to define sexual harassment.[7] The EEOC Guidelines describe "sexual harassment" as "unwelcome sexual advances, requests for sexual favors, and other verbal or physical conduct of a sexual nature [as] sexual harassment when this conduct explicitly or implicitly affects an individual's employment, unreasonably interferes with an individual's work performance, or creates an intimidating, hostile, or offensive work environment." In cases where the OIG believed the misconduct did not rise to the level of sexual harassment, we categorized the conduct as "Inappropriate Sexual Comments and/or Gestures," which comprise minor forms of the types of behavior described above.

Department policy prohibits sexual harassment of employees, which, like other forms of harassment, interferes with a productive

---

[6] FBI Offense Code 5.20, Sexual Misconduct.

[7] The legal framework protecting federal employees from harassment on the basis of sex, including employees of the law enforcement components, is contained in Section 703 of Title VII of the *Civil Rights Act of 1964*, the *Civil Service Reform Act of 1978*, and 29 C.F.R. § 1604.11 (which contains the Equal Employment Opportunity Commission's (EEOC) *Guidelines on Discrimination Because of Sex*) (hereinafter "EEOC Guidelines").

working environment, interjects irrelevant considerations into personnel decisions, and generally demeans the victims of harassment. Further, the law enforcement components developed policy in response to a 1993 mandate from the Attorney General to address this serious form of misconduct.[8] Appendix 4 contains information about the number of sexual misconduct and sexual harassment allegations opened during fiscal year (FY) 2009 through FY 2012 by offense category.

The Disciplinary Process

The legal framework governing the discipline of most federal service employees is contained in 5 U.S.C. Chapter 75 and 5 C.F.R. Part 752.[9] Additional policies and procedures directing how the Department handles discipline and adverse actions can be found in Department of Justice Order 1200.1.[10] This Order outlines the roles and responsibilities of management officials seeking to impose formal discipline and describes the mechanics of the inquiry, notice, adjudication, and grievance process applicable to most Department employees.

The Order also outlines the rights of employees who appeal their discipline in administrative proceedings before the Merit Systems Protection Board (MSPB) or mediate the decision in binding arbitration.[11] Although the laws and regulations described above provide the general framework for Department disciplinary systems, it is within the component's discretion to tailor its system to meet its organizational needs.

---

[8] *See* Memorandum on Prevention of Sexual Harassment in the Workplace, Attorney General, Janet Reno, June 29, 1993, as amended, December 14, 1998. *See also* ATF Order 2130.1A, *Conduct and Accountability, Section 14 Discrimination and Harassment,* February 7, 2012; DEA *Policy Statement on Sexual Harassment in the Workplace,* June 13, 2011; FBI *Policy on Harassment,* February 14, 2005; and the USMS *Equal Employment Opportunity Policy Statement,* May 3, 2012.

[9] 5 U.S.C. §§ 7501-7504, 7511-7514 (2009); 5 C.F.R. § 752.201-752.606 (2009).

[10] DOJ Order 1200.1, Chapter 3-1, Discipline and Adverse Actions (August 25, 1998).

[11] The MSPB is an independent, quasi-judicial agency in the Executive Branch that was established by Reorganization Plan No. 2 of 1978, which was codified by the *Civil Service Reform Act of 1978,* Pub. L. No. 95-454, 92 Stat. 1111 (CSRA). The CSRA authorized the MSPB to hear appeals of various agency decisions, most of which are appeals from agencies' adverse employment actions.

Unlike ATF, DEA, and USMS employees, the procedural protections described above do not apply to most FBI employees.[12] For example, unlike most other federal employees, FBI employees cannot appeal disciplinary decisions to the MSPB. (See 5 U.S.C. § 7511(b)(8)). Instead, the FBI has established an internal process for employees to appeal discipline decisions.

All non-frivolous allegations of criminal wrongdoing or serious administrative misconduct by Department employees must be reported to the OIG.[13]

The disciplinary processes of all four law enforcement components follow a similar format containing three distinct phases: reporting, investigation, and adjudication. For a detailed description of each component's disciplinary process, see Appendix 2.

---

[12] FBI employees to whom these procedural protections apply during the disciplinary process include preference-eligible veterans (5 U.S.C. § 7511(a)(1)(B)). Veterans are preference eligible if they are disabled or served on active duty during certain specified time periods or in military campaigns (5 U.S.C. § 2108).

[13] The OIG generally will investigate allegations of criminal or serious administrative misconduct, or misconduct by high-ranking employees or others as to which the impartiality of an internal investigation might be open to question. For the cases that the OIG investigates, the OIG issues a final report of investigation that is provided to the component, in order that the report can be used as the basis for the component's disciplinary decision.

See generally 28 C.F.R. Parts 0 and 45, which require the law enforcement components to refer all non-frivolous allegations of employee misconduct to the OIG. See also the Inspector General Act of 1978, as amended, 5 U.S.C. App § 8(E) (b) (2) (providing the Inspector General the authority to investigate any Department employee misconduct).

SCOPE AND METHODOLOGY OF THE OIG REVIEW

Scope

This review covered allegations of sexual misconduct and sexual harassment by law enforcement component employees from FY 2009 through FY 2012 (October 1, 2008 through September 30, 2012) that resulted in disciplinary action or decisions to take no action. We also included available information regarding misconduct allegations from this timeframe that were still open as of April 23, 2013, and updated the information during the course of our review.[14]

Methodology

Our review included data analysis, case file reviews, and interviews.[15] We reviewed applicable laws, regulations, policy, and written procedures related to the disciplinary process, sexual misconduct and sexual harassment. We collected and analyzed misconduct data and case files we received from the law enforcement components and from the OIG's Investigations Division.

Data Analyses and Case File Reviews

In April 2013, during the planning stages of this review, the OIG requested from the four Department law enforcement components all misconduct allegations from FY 2009 through FY 2012. ATF and the USMS readily provided this information, which assisted the OIG in determining what sexual misconduct and sexual harassment allegations would be within the scope of our review. By contrast, the DEA and the FBI initially stated they were unwilling to provide the OIG with information regarding such misconduct allegations until the OIG formally initiated the review. Both components cited the *Privacy Act* and concerns for the parties involved as the basis for not providing the

---

[14] Any open allegations of sexual misconduct or sexual harassment discussed in this report were monitored or investigated by the OIG. This review examines the policies and processes employed by the law enforcement components, and not the OIG's investigation or monitoring of the underlying matters.

[15] Component case files may contain multiple allegations against multiple subjects. For purposes of this review, we generally count each case file as a separate case and each subject of an investigation as a separate allegation. However, during adjudication, an adjudicative case file contains only information relating to an individual subject. Therefore, when discussing the adjudicative process, we refer to each subject as a case.

information.[16] We had to elevate these issues for discussion with the respective component senior management.

The following sections discuss what occurred with data requests made to the FBI and DEA.

FBI data requests: In order to identify sexual misconduct and harassment cases within our scope, we initially provided the FBI with a list of search terms to use in its database queries. In consultation with the OIG, the FBI developed a shorter list of search terms that focused on seven offense categories relating to sexual misconduct and sexual harassment. However, when the FBI provided the results of their searches, the information it provided was heavily redacted and prevented the OIG from understanding the nature and circumstances of the allegations.

When we questioned the inadequate nature of these productions, the FBI continued to raise unsupportable objections related to the *Privacy Act* to producing unredacted materials to the OIG. It was not until August 2013 that the FBI agreed to provide the OIG with case files.

To help ensure that we had received all cases within the scope of our review from the FBI, we ran a search of the OIG Investigation Division's database with our full list of search terms. We then evaluated the search results to determine which cases were within the scope of our review, and we compared those cases with what we received from the FBI. Through this process, we found a material number of additional allegations of sexual misconduct and sexual harassment that were not included in FBI's productions. We requested and ultimately received information from the FBI on these additional cases.

Also, based upon our analysis of the FBI's search process, we determined that a significant number of cases were within the scope of our review and met the agreed upon FBI search criteria, but were not provided to the OIG. As a result of these initially incomplete productions, we cannot be confident that the FBI provided us with all of

---

[16] This refusal was puzzling to us, given that the OIG is an organization within the Department and that the OIG routinely handles information it receives from Department components consistent with the *Privacy Act*. Furthermore, the OIG Investigations Division receives from these same law enforcement components all such misconduct allegations on a regular basis, though not with all the same information and disciplinary outcomes necessary for this review. *See generally* 28 C.F.R. Parts 0 and 45, which require the law enforcement components to refer all non-frivolous allegations of employee misconduct to the OIG. *See also* the *Inspector General Act of 1978,* as amended, 5 U.S.C. App § 8(E) (b) (2) (providing the Inspector General the authority to investigate any Department employee misconduct).

the relevant information necessary for our review. Moreover, the failure to provide case file information in a timely fashion unnecessarily delayed our work. Therefore, our report reflects the findings and conclusions we reached based on the information made available to us. For a more detailed discussion regarding the allegations we reviewed for each of the law enforcement components, see Appendix 1.

DEA data requests: In order to identify sexual misconduct and harassment cases within our scope, we initially provided the DEA with a list of search terms to use in its database queries. The DEA did not provide the OIG with case file information until several months after we first requested it, and only after we formally initiated the review. Moreover, in August 2013, when the DEA provided the OIG with case file information, the information was so heavily redacted that it prevented the OIG from understanding the nature and circumstances of the allegations.[17] When we questioned the inadequate nature of these productions, the DEA continued to raise unsupportable objections related to the *Privacy Act* to producing unredacted materials to the OIG. It was not until September 2013 that the DEA provided mostly unredacted case file information, but it continued to redact some relevant information.

To help ensure that we had received all cases within the scope of our review from the DEA, we ran a search of the OIG Investigation Division's database with our full list of search terms. We then evaluated the search results to determine which cases were within the scope of our review, and we compared those cases with what we received from the DEA. Through this process, we found a material number of additional allegations of sexual misconduct and sexual harassment that were not included in DEA's productions. We requested and ultimately received information from the DEA on these additional cases.

Moreover, in November 2014, after a working draft of our report was issued to the components, we learned for the first time that the DEA had not run the full list of search terms provided by the OIG. Instead, the DEA informed us that it had run only three search terms related to sexual misconduct and harassment and initially provided the OIG with a more limited number of cases as a result. Based upon our analysis of the DEA's search process, we determined that a significant number of cases were within the scope of our review and met the DEA-selected search criteria, but were not provided to the OIG during their initial production.

---

[17] For an example of the redacted information provided by DEA during this phase of our review, see Appendix 6.

Because of these initially incomplete productions, we cannot be confident that the DEA provided us with all of the relevant information necessary for our review. Moreover, the failure to provide case file information in a timely fashion unnecessarily delayed our work. Therefore, our report reflects the findings and conclusions we reached based on the information made available to us. For a more detailed discussion regarding the allegations we reviewed for each of the law enforcement components, see Appendix 1.

Interviews

We interviewed officials and staff members responsible for the reporting, investigation, and adjudication of discipline and adverse actions at the law enforcement components. We also interviewed staff members in their respective Chief or General Counsel's Offices. Further, we interviewed the components' security personnel and information technology personnel, the Department's Security and Emergency Planning Staff (SEPS), and personnel from the Office of the Deputy Attorney General.

We were concerned by an apparent decision by DEA to withhold information regarding an open matter during our initial interviews with several DEA employees. When we re-interviewed these employees after the DEA provided the case file following its closure, the employees stated they were given the impression by DEA that they were not to discuss the case with the OIG while the case remained open. The OIG was entitled to receive all such information from the outset of our review. The failure to provide it in a timely fashion unnecessarily delayed our work.

The next section of the report discusses the results of the review. Chapter 1 discusses the reporting of allegations of sexual misconduct and sexual harassment. Chapter 2 discusses the security of operations, while Chapters 3 and 4 discuss the investigation and adjudication of sexual misconduct and sexual harassment allegations. Chapter 5 discusses detecting and retaining sexually explicit text message evidence.

CHAPTER 1: THE REPORTING PROCESS

Although the ATF and the USMS have clear policies requiring supervisors to report misconduct allegations, including alleged sexual misconduct and sexual harassment, to their headquarters internal affairs offices, we found that supervisors sometimes failed to report these allegations, even when the subject was alleged to have committed similar misconduct in the past.

At the DEA and the FBI, we found their misconduct reporting policies did not clearly delineate what should be reported to headquarters and what should be treated as a local management or performance-related issue. We found that, as a result, supervisors at these components exercised discretion in deciding what to report, even when their respective offense tables characterized sexual misconduct and sexual harassment as prohibited behavior.

As a result, in all four components, allegations were not reported by their headquarters to the OIG when they first occurred, and in some cases, even some repeated allegations of sexual misconduct or sexual harassment may not have been fully investigated.

ATF

ATF Order 2130.A, *Conduct and Accountability*, requires ATF managers, supervisors, and employees to report to Internal Affairs Division (IAD) at ATF headquarters all suspected or alleged incidents of misconduct related to integrity, professionalism, and impartiality.[18] ATF Order 8610.B, *Integrity and Other Investigations*, also requires ATF employees to promptly report any allegation or information indicating a violation of the standards of conduct (both government-wide or ATF standards), a violation of any Department rule, or any criminal conduct to their supervisor, IAD, or directly to the Department of Justice (DOJ) OIG.

We found that in 4 of the 47 allegations (8.5 percent) we reviewed, ATF supervisors failed to report allegations of sexual misconduct and

---

[18] For purposes of this report, the OIG does not make a distinction between sexual misconduct and misconduct related to integrity, professionalism, and impartiality. Sexual misconduct, to include matters relating to sexual harassment, can and often does relate directly to integrity, professionalism, and impartiality.

sexual harassment to the Internal Affairs Division (IAD) as ATF policy required and instead handled matters locally. In these cases, the subjects who committed the alleged misconduct continued to engage in prohibited behavior and the OIG did not learn about the alleged misconduct when it first occurred.

Case #1: For over 3 years, an ATF Program Manager failed to report allegations that two training instructors were having consensual sex with their students. According to the incident report, the Program Manager learned the same instructors had engaged in substantially the same activities 3 years earlier but had merely counseled the training instructors without reporting the alleged activities to the IAD. When division management learned about the latest incident from the Program Manager, they reported the matter to the IAD, and the Program Manager cancelled the instructors' contracts and removed them from their positions.[19]

Based on our review of the case file, we concluded the Program Manager did not comply with ATF policy requiring managers to report to the IAD all suspected or alleged incidents of misconduct related to integrity, professionalism, and impartiality. In addition, the Program Manager's failure to report the alleged misconduct when it first occurred prevented the IAD from referring the allegations to the OIG when they were first discovered. There is no indication in the case file that the Program Manager was investigated for failing to report the first incident.

Case #2: A Special Agent in Charge (SAC) and an Assistant Special Agent in Charge (ASAC) failed to promptly report allegations of an inappropriate relationship between the ASAC and a subordinate and the intentional misuse of government vehicles to facilitate that relationship. The subordinate's spouse, who was also an ATF employee, insisted the ASAC report the relationship to local ATF management. Once it was reported, the subordinate was removed from the ASAC's supervision; however, the SAC treated the romantic relationship as a "management issue" and did not report the matter to the IAD. The matter ultimately was reported to the IAD following additional allegations that the subordinate had engaged in similar misconduct. The ASAC ultimately received a 45-day suspension for misusing a government vehicle and for failing to report the subordinate's continued use of the government

---

[19] ATF does not have any additional information indicating that the instructors appealed the termination of their contracts. However, one of the instructors was re-instituted and ATF has subsequently utilized that instructor for two task orders. ATF stated that this instructor's actions were not as egregious as the other individual. ATF personnel also stated that the decision to not use the other instructor was due to the totality of the circumstances involving the disciplinary matter.

vehicle to facilitate the relationship. The subordinate also received a 30-day suspension for misuse of a government vehicle.

We found that the SAC and the ASAC did not comply with ATF policy by failing to promptly report the relationship and the misuse of a government vehicle. Although the ASAC eventually was disciplined for failing to report the subordinate's government vehicle misuse, the SAC retired and was not investigated or disciplined for failing to report these matters. Further, the IAD was unable to refer the allegations to the OIG when they were first discovered because the SAC and the ASAC did not report them.

DEA

We found that the DEA lacks clear policy on whether to report alleged misconduct to headquarters and the DEA provides supervisors discretion when deciding whether to do so. We determined that in 10 of the 113 allegations (9 percent), DEA supervisors failed to report allegations of sexual misconduct and sexual harassment through their chain of command or to the DEA's Office of Professional Responsibility (OPR). In these instances, DEA supervisors treated alleged sexual misconduct and sexual harassment as a local management or performance-related issue. As a result, the OIG did not learn about the alleged misconduct and was unable to review the allegations when they first arose.

The DEA *Personnel Manual*, Section 2735.1, *Standards of Conduct*, requires DEA employees to promptly report to their supervisor or directly to the DEA OPR any information that indicates or alleges that another DEA employee engaged in improper or illegal activities in violation of the DEA *Standards of Conduct*. However, DEA supervisors have discretion when determining whether the reported matter is a management or performance-related issue that can be handled locally or whether it is misconduct requiring a report to DEA OPR. Where there is a question about how the matter should be handled, the DEA *Personnel Manual* advises supervisors to consult with their chain of command or DEA OPR. However, DEA supervisors are not required to do so.

The DEA *Guide of Disciplinary Offenses and Penalties* also contains descriptions of various types of prohibited behavior and puts employees and supervisors on notice as to what constitutes misconduct. Even though the reporting policy contained in the *Personnel Manual* lacks clarity, the DEA offense table and the *Standards of Conduct* provide some guidance to supervisors and employees.

We found instances where it appears that due to a lack of clear policy, sexual misconduct and sexual harassment allegations were either not being reported to DEA OPR when they were first discovered or were not reported at all. In these cases, DEA supervisors treated the alleged misconduct as a local management issue. We discuss two cases below.

Case #1: We found that a Regional Director, an Acting Assistant Regional Director (AARD), and a Group Supervisor failed to report through their chain of command or to the DEA OPR repeated allegations of DEA Special Agents (SA) patronizing prostitutes and frequenting a brothel while in an overseas posting, treating these allegations as local management issues.[20] It was also alleged that one of the subjects in the supervisors' group assaulted a prostitute following a payment dispute. The matter ultimately was reported to the DEA OPR in June 2010 in an anonymous letter alleging that two Special Agents had frequented prostitutes while in an overseas posting on a regular basis.

According to DEA OPR's report of investigation, the agents' in-country supervisors were aware of several loud parties with prostitutes that occurred at a Special Agent's government-leased quarters, because the Special Agent had received four complaint letters from building management, who had also informed local DEA management about the complaints between August 2005 and December 2008. In subsequent interviews with DEA OPR, this SA said that a Group Supervisor, the Regional Director, and the Acting Assistant Regional Director had warned the SA to discontinue the parties or be removed from the overseas assignment. However, they did not inform DEA OPR about the allegations.

According to the case file, the Regional Director justified the failure to report the allegations by stating that the matter was a management issue. When the DEA OPR questioned whether the Regional Director failed to report an OPR matter, the Regional Director stated he believed the matter "was under the immediate purview of the Regional Security Officer" and "was being reviewed by competent and independent authority." The DEA OPR reported the matter to the DEA Administrator and, in 2012, the DEA Administrator counseled the Regional Director for failing to report the allegations. The Acting Assistant Regional Director and Group Supervisor were not subjects of the separate investigation

---

[20] The Acting Assistant Regional Director who supervised the two special agents in this case was also alleged to have solicited prostitutes in the DEA case we discuss in Chapter 2, Security of Operations. In that case, the AARD allegedly engaged in sexual relations with prostitutes at a farewell party in the AARD's honor. There were also allegations operational funds were used to pay for the party and the prostitutes who participated.

and were not disciplined, and the SA whose quarters were used for the parties received a 14-day suspension for Conduct Unbecoming a DEA Agent and Improper Association.

Even though the DEA's reporting policy affords some discretion to DEA supervisors on whether to report alleged misconduct to the OPR or whether to handle it locally, the alleged misconduct described above clearly should have been reported to the DEA OPR because it falls within the offense category *Criminal, Dishonest, Infamous or Notoriously Disgraceful Conduct* that is contrary to the DEA *Standards of Conduct* and is prohibited in its offense table. For the Regional Director to have treated such conduct as a local management issue is troubling. Further, the supervisors' failure to promptly report the alleged misconduct prevented the DEA OPR from referring these allegations to the OIG for investigation when they were first discovered.

Case #2: In another case, a DEA Country Attaché and Group Supervisor failed to report repeated incidents of sexual harassment and other misconduct through their chain of command or to DEA OPR. According to the OPR case file, in May 2010, DEA received a complaint through the Department of State, Diplomatic Security Service, regarding an Assistant Regional Director (ARD) in an overseas Country Office. According to the report of investigation, a Foreign Service National (FSN) who served as the ARD's Assistant alleged that the ARD made numerous inappropriate sexual comments; asked the FSN to watch pornographic movies; and routinely threw items, yelled at employees, and used other vulgarities in the office and at official functions, among other allegations.[21]

When a second employee raised concerns about the ARD's behavior to the Country Attaché and the Group Supervisor, they told the second employee to discontinue any direct contact with the ARD but did not report the allegations to DEA OPR. Ultimately, after the FSN's complaint to the Embassy's Regional Security Office was referred through the State Department to the DEA OPR, the ARD received a letter of reprimand for Failure to Follow Instructions and Conduct Unbecoming a DEA Agent for using profanity, yelling, and throwing things in the office.

---

[21] DEA did not provide the OIG with the allegations contained in Case #2. We discovered them with the assistance of the OIG Investigations Division. The allegation was not investigated or monitored by the OIG, but was referred back to the DEA OPR to investigate as a management referral.

Even though the DEA's reporting policy affords some discretion to DEA supervisors on whether to report alleged misconduct to the DEA OPR or whether to handle it locally, we found the alleged misconduct described above warranted a report to the DEA OPR, rather than treating such conduct locally as a management issue. Such conduct is contrary to the DEA *Standards of Conduct* and is prohibited in the offense table, thus warranting a referral to the DEA OPR.

The fact that the alleged misconduct involved executive management could have indicated to employees in the field that the ARD's behavior was acceptable and tolerated by the supervisors in this country office, underscoring that local office management were not the appropriate individuals to handle these issues. Further, the supervisors' failure to promptly report these allegations prevented the DEA OPR from referring the alleged misconduct to the OIG when they were first discovered.

FBI

The FBI also lacks clear policy on whether to report alleged misconduct to headquarters and provides FBI supervisors with discretion when making these determinations. We found that, as a result, in 32 of the 258 allegations (approximately 12 percent) we reviewed, FBI supervisors failed to report allegations of sexual misconduct and sexual harassment to the Inspection Division, Internal Investigations Section. In these instances, FBI supervisors treated alleged sexual misconduct and sexual harassment as local management issues. Further, the OIG would not learn about the alleged misconduct in order to be able to review it when it first occurred.

According to the FBI Code of Conduct, "FBI employees shall report to the proper authority any violations of law and regulation by themselves or others." The FBI *Offense Codes and Penalties Guidelines* contains descriptions of prohibited behavior and includes an offense category requiring FBI employees to report to the appropriate FBI official or supervisor in a timely manner allegations of administrative or criminal misconduct which the employee knew or should have known to be a violation of FBI or DOJ regulation or policy. In interviews, Internal Investigations Section (IIS) management told us that all misconduct allegations must be reported to IIS for a determination as to whether the alleged misconduct warranted investigation because the IIS staff are the subject matter experts.

However, the *Internal Investigations Section Supervisor's Guide* provides FBI supervisors and senior management with more discretion when determining whether to report misconduct allegations to headquarters, requiring only the reporting of "all allegations of employee serious misconduct or criminality."

The *IIS Supervisor's Guide* also advises supervisors to refer to the FBI *Offense Codes and Penalty Guidelines*, which describes various types of prohibited behavior, when determining what types of alleged misconduct warrant referral to the IIS Initial Processing Unit (IPU). When there is doubt, the Guide advises supervisors to contact the IPU Unit Chief or the Lead Conduct Review Specialist by telephone for guidance in evaluating whether an allegation warrants a referral. We therefore concluded that the FBI policy on reporting misconduct allegations to the IIS still leaves local supervisors with discretion in deciding whether to report misconduct.

In contrast to sexual misconduct, the FBI has a specific reporting policy regarding sexual harassment.[22] It states that once a sexual harassment incident has been reported, "the supervisor must take immediate corrective action and must also report the allegations of sexual harassment to the Inspection Division, Internal Investigations Section, as potential employee misconduct."

We found instances where it appeared that, because the policy on reporting sexual misconduct is unclear, the discretion given to FBI supervisors resulted in such allegations not being reported to the FBI IIS when they were first discovered or that they were never reported. We also found sexual harassment allegations that were not reported to the FBI IIS when they were first discovered or were never reported despite the FBI's clear policy requiring reporting of these matters. Also, even after this failure to report was discovered by the FBI IIS, it did not open an investigation into the failure to report. We discuss two sexual harassment cases with reporting issues below.

Case #1: A line supervisor, an Assistant Section Chief, a Section Chief, and an Assistant Director failed to report a Supervisory Management and Program Analyst's (SMAPA) repeated unprofessional behavior, including cornering his subordinates in their cubicles and displaying the size of his genitals by tightening his pants, making graphic and inappropriate sexual comments and gestures, and otherwise creating a hostile work environment.

Instead of reporting this conduct to headquarters, the supervisors counseled the SMAPA on four occasions and, in the last session, required the SMAPA to sign a document in which the SMAPA pledged to refrain

---

[22] FBI Policy on Harassment, dated February 14, 2005.

from such conduct. Even after signing the document, the SMAPA continued to engage in the misconduct, at which point the Assistant Director reported it to the IIS. Accordingly, the subordinates experienced the SMAPA's misconduct for approximately 3 years before it was reported to headquarters.

According to the case file, two of the subordinates said they reported the SMAPA's conduct to the Assistant Section Chiefs and the Section Chief of their division on several occasions, but they seemed "unsupportive and unconcerned." In interviews with IIS, one Assistant Section Chief commented that the SMAPA's personal relationships with the Section Chief and the other Assistant Section Chief were the main reason why they were unconcerned and failed to take appropriate action. Ultimately, the SMAPA received a 60-day suspension for Unprofessional Conduct – On Duty and Insubordination, was demoted to a non-supervisory position, and was reassigned to another office. Although the Section Chief was also a subject of the investigation, no disciplinary action was taken.

We concluded that the supervisors in this case should have reported the allegations when they first occurred, rather than treating such repeated and egregious misconduct as a local management issue. The allegations that the SMAPA made repeated inappropriate sexual comments and advances to multiple subordinates falls within *Offense Code 5.20, Sexual Harassment,* described as "making unwelcome or unwanted sexual advances, requesting sexual favors, or engaging in other verbal or physical conduct of a sexual nature."

The impressions that the Section Chief and the Assistant Section Chief were "unsupportive and unconcerned" about the SMAPA's alleged conduct and the belief of at least one other Assistant Section Chief that the handling of the matter was influenced by their personal relationship with the subject provide additional evidence for why the allegations should have been referred to headquarters at the outset. Further, the division management's failure to promptly report the alleged misconduct prevented the IIS from referring these allegations to the OIG for possible investigation when they were first discovered.

Case #2: In another case, FBI supervisors counseled a subject twice before reporting alleged sexual harassment to the IIS. According to the IIS case file, in December 2008, an FBI Training Assistant reported that a probationary Fingerprint Examiner was making unwanted sexual advances toward the Assistant. The misconduct began in November 2008, when the Fingerprint Examiner (the subject) requested a private meeting with the Assistant and, despite being married, confessed an infatuation with the Assistant. The subject sent numerous e-mails and

16

text messages to the Assistant, who expressed disinterest in pursuing a relationship. However, the subject persisted, discussed in e-mail his plans to leave his wife, and wrote that he turned down sexual relations with his spouse because of the unrequited infatuation with the Assistant. The Assistant reported these concerns to first-line supervisors, and they counseled the subject but did not notify the IIS. The subject admitted the misconduct and apologized to the Assistant.

Despite the initial counseling session and the subject's admission and apology to the Assistant, the subject continued to make unwanted advances. In January 2009, the Assistant made another report to first-line supervisors alleging continued unwanted advances, and they again counseled the subject without notifying the IIS. The supervisors also moved the subject's workspace from the immediate proximity of the Assistant and provided him with a copy of the FBI's Sexual Harassment Policy.

In February 2009, the first-line supervisors reported the allegations to the division's executive management, who met with the subject and decided to report the matter to the IIS. In the electronic communication to the IIS, the reporting division described the situation as "deplorable and unacceptable," though they indicated that they believed their prior course of action was appropriate because the subject was a probationary employee who was being transferred to another unit.[23]

We concluded that even though the FBI's reporting policy leaves discretion as to reporting allegations to IIS, the supervisors should have reported the incidents described above to the FBI IIS when they first occurred, rather than treating such conduct as a management issue. Despite division management's attempts to rectify the situation through counseling, there was e-mail and text message evidence that documented the subject's continued unrequited sexual advances, conduct that is clearly prohibited by FBI *Offense Code 5.20, Sexual Harassment.*

In addition, the FBI offense table does not designate sexual harassment as an offense warranting investigation in the field rather than at headquarters. According to the *IIS Supervisor's Guide,* offenses designated as Delegated Investigation Only (DIO) or Delegated

---

[23] The IIS did not investigate the matter but agreed to monitor the situation, instructing the reporting division to make an immediate report if any other developments materialized, and the employee was not disciplined. By failing to take action, there is a risk that other FBI employees may experience the misconduct alleged by the Assistant.

Investigation Adjudication (DIA) are investigated and, if appropriate, adjudicated by supervisors and Assistant Inspectors In Place (AIIP) in the field. Typically, property-related and general misconduct allegations are designated as DIO, DIA, or both. Because the alleged misconduct fell within the *Sexual Harassment* offense category, however, an immediate report to the IIS was warranted. Further, we found the supervisors' failure to promptly report the alleged misconduct prevented the IIS from referring these allegations to the OIG for possible investigation when they were first discovered.

USMS

We found that in 9 of the 81 allegations (11 percent) we reviewed, USMS supervisors failed to report allegations of sexual misconduct and sexual harassment to the Office of Professional Responsibility, Internal Affairs (OPR-IA) as required by policy, and instead handled matters in the field. The OIG did not learn about the alleged misconduct when it first occurred.

According to USMS Policy Directive 3.3, *Performance & Related Matters, Human Resources, Discipline and Adverse Actions,* USMS supervisors are required "to promptly report, through channels, to the OPR-IA alleged infractions of statutes or regulations or other misconduct that may warrant discipline." In interviews, OPR-IA officials stated that supervisors in the field must report all alleged misconduct or criminal activity, whether on duty or off, to headquarters. Despite this clear directive, we found instances where the allegations were not reported when they were first discovered. We discuss two cases below.

Case #1: A USMS supervisor failed to promptly report allegations that a Deputy U.S. Marshal (DUSM) solicited prostitutes while on an extradition mission in Bangkok, Thailand. According to the case file, the supervisor learned about the allegations when the DUSM's colleague reported the matter to management. At that time, the supervisor met with the DUSM; the DUSM admitted the misconduct and received an oral admonishment.

The USMS OPR-IA learned about the allegation when the State Department referred the allegation to the OIG and the OIG notified the OPR-IA. In an e-mail to OPR-IA, the supervisor explained that the allegation was not reported to the OPR-IA at the outset because no formal complaint was made against the DUSM.[24]

---

[24] Ultimately, the OPR-IA administratively closed the allegation and referred the allegation back to the originating district. The supervisor took no further action, and the matter was closed.

In an interview with the OIG, the supervisor expressed the belief that the DUSM's conduct was not misconduct but simply amounted to a personal indiscretion and that handling the matter internally seemed appropriate at the time. However, the supervisor admitted that the failure to report was an error in judgment, stating, "The only thing I would've regretted about how I handled this, was that I did not call internal first." We determined that the supervisor was not investigated or disciplined for failing to report the matter. The supervisor reportedly notified the U.S. Marshal, who also did not report the allegations to the OPR-IA.

We found that the district management's failure to promptly report these allegations violated the USMS policy requiring all employees to report allegations of misconduct, whether on duty or off. Although the OIG ultimately learned about this incident through a State Department referral, it was the district management's responsibility to report these allegations to OPR-IA when they first were received.

Case #2: An Acting Supervisory Deputy U.S. Marshal (SDUSM) reported to district executive management allegations that a DUSM had an inappropriate relationship with the common law spouse of a fugitive. However, the Acting Chief Deputy U.S. Marshal, other district executive management, and a representative of the Office of General Counsel (OGC) failed to report these matters to OPR-IA and instead counseled the DUSM.

According to the OPR-IA report of investigation, an Acting SDUSM learned that a Deputy U.S. Marshal had entered into a romantic relationship with the common law spouse of a USMS fugitive. The Acting SDUSM contacted the USMS Office of General Counsel, Acting Chief Deputy U.S. Marshal, and another SDUSM in the district to determine how to handle the situation. Three supervisors instructed the DUSM to terminate the relationship, but the DUSM continued to pursue it without their knowledge for approximately 1 year. Neither the supervisors nor the OGC representative with whom they consulted reported the allegations to the OPR-IA.

When the relationship ended, the fugitive's spouse lodged a complaint with the OIG, which referred the allegation back to USMS OPR-IA for handling as a management referral.[25]

---

[25] The DUSM was removed for the misconduct but appealed to the Merit Systems Protection Board and reached a settlement, allowing the DUSM to resign.

Although the Acting SDUSM reported the matter through the chain of command when the incident was first discovered and the Acting SDUSM sought guidance from OGC on how to handle the issue, both district management and the OGC failed to promptly report these allegations to the OPR-IA. This also resulted in the OIG not learning about the misconduct when the allegation was first discovered.

In the next chapter, we discuss issues that we discovered in the security process.

CHAPTER 2: SECURITY OF OPERATIONS

At ATF, DEA, and USMS, we found there is a lack of coordination between the internal affairs offices that investigate sexual misconduct allegations and the offices responsible for ensuring employees meet the requirements to hold security clearances, despite explicit policies requiring such coordination. We determined that in most cases where internal affairs received allegations that employees reportedly engaged in high-risk sexual behavior, security personnel were not informed about these incidents until well after they occurred or were never informed.[26] This was true even though these three components each have policies requiring some coordination between their internal affairs and security personnel and even though such behavior has the potential to expose the employees to coercion, extortion, and blackmail, presenting serious security risks for the components.

By contrast with the other three law enforcement components, we found that the FBI has taken a better approach to addressing such potential security issues and we determined that all misconduct allegations were referred to FBI security personnel for review. Specifically, the FBI Internal Investigations Section refers all misconduct allegations to the Security Division, Analysis and Investigations Unit (AIU) for a determination as to whether the allegation raises security risks for the FBI or whether the allegation raises concerns about the employee's continued eligibility to hold a security clearance. If these risks are present, AIU opens a parallel investigation.

ATF, the DEA, and the USMS have delegated authority from the Department's Security and Emergency Planning Staff to grant National Security Information (NSI) Clearances up to the Top Secret level, while FBI has independent statutory authority to adjudicate to the Top Secret level. At all the components, if a higher security clearance is required, the SEPS adjudicates the clearance.

---

[26] High-risk sexual behavior involves a criminal offense, indicates a personality or emotional disorder, reflects lack of judgment or discretion, or may subject the individual to undue influence or coercion, exploitation, or duress can raise questions about an individual's reliability, trustworthiness, and ability to protect classified information.

The law enforcement components are required to ensure their employees' initial and continued eligibility for access to classified information. Security personnel throughout the federal government use the *Adjudicative Guidelines for Determining Eligibility for Access to Classified Information* (Guidelines) to make these determinations.[27]

The Guidelines are comprised of three parts: the concern, the potentially disqualifying conditions, and mitigating factors. There are 13 areas of concern described in the Guidelines. Specifically, Adjudicative Guideline D: "Sexual Behavior" outlines various types of sexual behavior security personnel should consider, including sexual behavior:

- of a criminal nature, whether or not the individual has been prosecuted;

- [that reflects] a pattern of compulsive, self-destructive, or high-risk sexual behavior that the person is unable to stop or that may be symptomatic of a personality disorder;

- that causes an individual to be vulnerable to coercion, exploitation, or duress; and

- of a public nature and/or that reflects lack of discretion or judgment.

Although ATF, the DEA, and the USMS have established policies requiring some level of coordination between their internal affairs offices and security personnel, we found this coordination did not always occur in practice. The following sections discuss the lack of coordination at ATF, the DEA, and the USMS.

ATF

Of the 40 sexual misconduct and sexual harassment cases, we found 3 substantiated cases and 1 administratively closed case involving high-risk sexual behavior where the Internal Affairs Division (IAD) failed to refer the allegations arising between fiscal year 2009 through fiscal year 2012 to the Personnel Security Branch (PSB) to determine if they

---

[27] The 13 areas of concern described in the Adjudicative Guidelines are: (A) Allegiance to the United States; (B) Foreign Influence; (C) Foreign Preference; (D) Sexual Behavior; (E) Personal Conduct; (F) Financial Considerations; (G) Alcohol Consumption; (H) Drug Involvement; (I) Psychological Conditions; (J) Criminal Conduct; (K) Handling Protected Information; (L) Outside Activities; and (M) Misuse of Information Technology. *See generally* Memorandum from Stephen J. Hadley, White House Assistant to the President for National Security Affairs, *Adjudicative Guidelines for Determining Eligibility for Access to Classified Information*, December 29, 2005.

presented potential security risks for ATF and for the employees involved.[28] We determined that this occurred because the IAD had not established a process for reporting misconduct allegations to the PSB. We concluded that because there was no process for notifying the PSB about misconduct allegations, the PSB was hampered in its ability to assess an employee's continued eligibility to hold a security clearance.

According to ATF Order 8610.B, the IAD must report to PSB any "conditions that could raise a security concern as defined by the ATF *Adjudicative Guidelines*."[29] Specifically, the IAD evaluates an allegation and drafts an incident report. Once the Assistant Director of Office of Professional Responsibility, Security Operations (OPRSO) reviews the allegation, the Order requires the OPRSO or the IAD to report any conditions that could raise a security concern to the PSB. If the PSB believes the employee's behavior is an area of concern under the *Adjudicative Guidelines,* the PSB may suspend an employee's eligibility for access to classified information, pending the conclusion of the IAD investigation.

In interviews, IAD and PSB officials told us that the IAD typically does not provide information to the PSB about current investigations where IAD does not believe that there is an immediate security risk, out of concern that doing so may compromise its work, particularly when the subject is not aware they are being investigated. PSB officials told us this is problematic because IAD is not familiar with the *Adjudicative Guidelines,* and IAD is not in the best position to determine whether an allegation poses a security risk.

PSB officials told us that they have made numerous attempts to establish a process for the referral of misconduct allegations raising security concerns, but a process had not been established during our review period. However, IAD officials stated that it was a priority of the

---

[28] An allegation is substantiated when it has gone through the entire disciplinary process, reporting, investigation, and adjudication, and the component has determined that the subject committed the alleged misconduct. The administratively closed case involved allegations that an ATF agent and evidence custodian failed to properly secure drug evidence. The case file also revealed allegations that the same ATF agent had inappropriate relationships with a particular female confidential informant (CI). Although ATF decided that the latter allegations did not warrant investigation, the agent's supervisor counseled the subject regarding his relationships with CIs. The substantiated cases involved an inappropriate relationship with a "criminal element" alleged to be a cocaine user, the arrest of an ATF employee for failing to pay for a visit to a massage parlor, and the solicitation of multiple consensual sexual partners by an ATF employee.

[29] The ATF's *Adjudicative Guidelines* are a restatement of the Adjudicative Guidelines applying to all federal employees holding a security clearance.

new management in the OPRSO to establish a process for referring misconduct allegations raising security concerns. At the time of our review, we found that PSB was made aware of an allegation only if it was self-reported, if the allegation received media attention, or if an employee involved in the disciplinary process decided to notify the PSB.[30] As a result, the PSB was not aware of all potential security risks as they arose.

In interviews, we also learned that, even when the IAD refers a matter to the PSB, the IAD may provide the PSB with only the proposal and decision letters once a misconduct case is adjudicated. According to PSB officials, the IAD routinely denied PSB access to the full IAD report of investigation when an allegation raised security concerns. Instead, IAD provided the proposal and decision letters issued to the employee, which we found often contained only a brief synopsis of the case and do not include important details that could be relevant to a determination regarding the appropriateness of an employee maintaining a security clearance. Other than citing general privacy concerns, IAD officials could not explain why they routinely do not provide the PSB with the reports of investigations.

One case in particular illustrates the importance of the need for sustained coordination between the PSB and the IAD on matters with potential security concerns. The case involved the solicitation of multiple consensual sexual partners by an ATF employee on temporary duty. This case is discussed in greater detail below.

Case Example: In November 2009, an ATF Director of Industry Operations (DIO) who holds a Top Secret security clearance was on temporary assignment. According to the IAD report of investigation, the DIO solicited consensual sex with anonymous partners and modified a hotel room door to facilitate sexual play. In addition, the DIO removed smoke detectors from the hotel room and inadvertently caused damage to the hotel's centralized fire detection system. When the hotel supervisor contacted the local police, the DIO admitted the conduct and told local police this type of conduct was not an isolated incident for him and had occurred in the past. The DIO pled guilty to one count of misdemeanor "fire prevention interference." The DIO was placed on inactive probation for 12 months and was ordered to pay a fine and court costs. The incident received significant media attention in the local area.

---

[30] As discussed in Appendix 2 of this report, the employees involved in the ATF disciplinary process are the: (1) Internal Affairs Division, (2) the Professional Review Board, and (3) the ATF Deciding Official.

Even though this conduct would clearly have been relevant under the Guidelines for determining the DIO's continued access to classified information, we found the Internal Affairs Division failed to notify the PSB about this case. The PSB became aware of the incident only when an employee in the office read a news article about the case over a year after the incident occurred, prior to which the DIO had maintained his security clearance without review. Once the PSB became aware of the matter, it requested the report of investigation from the IAD.

In interviews, we learned that the IAD would not provide the report of investigation to the PSB and provided only the proposal and decision letters. The proposal and decision letters described the incident but failed to describe the pattern of high-risk sexual behavior discussed in the report, specifically including the DIO's admission that he had engaged in such conduct before. Ultimately, the DIO received a 14-day suspension for the misconduct described above and will be subject to additional scrutiny during the DIO's 5-year reinvestigation.

In interviews, PSB staff told us the DIO's conduct is an area of concern identified in the *Adjudicative Guideline* on Sexual Behavior, specifically described as a "pattern of compulsive, self-destructive, or high-risk sexual behavior that the person is unable to stop." According to the Guideline, consensual sex with anonymous partners is also an area of concern, particularly where it is "of a public nature and/or that reflects lack of discretion or judgment." The PSB told us the DIO's admission that this type of conduct was not isolated and had occurred in the past warranted a review of the DIO's Top Secret clearance. However, this did not occur because the PSB did not receive the report of investigation containing the admission.

We concluded that this case highlights how a failure by the IAD to refer misconduct allegations to the PSB as they arise can prevent ATF from addressing security threats in a timely fashion. To mitigate these risks, we believe that all non-frivolous misconduct allegations involving ATF employees should be referred to the PSB when they arise and that the report of investigation should be included, when available. If referring the allegation has the potential to compromise an IAD investigation, the referral should still be made to PSB to allow security personnel to monitor the situation while not discussing the potential security violations with the employee until the IAD investigation is completed or it agrees with IAD that notification of the employee is no longer an issue. As a result of this review, the ATF has informed us that a policy has been issued which will improve the coordination between ATF IAD and ATF PSB.

DEA

Of the 77 sexual misconduct and sexual harassment cases we reviewed, we found 6 substantiated cases during our review period involving high-risk sexual behavior, among other things, where the DEA Office of Professional Responsibility (OPR) failed to refer the allegations to the Office of Security Programs (OSP).[31]

According to the *DEA Office of Professional Responsibility Handbook*, while conducting a preliminary inquiry and throughout the investigation process of allegations of misconduct, OPR Inspectors are required to evaluate whether a misconduct allegation raises security concerns or whether the allegation compromises the employee's continued ability to hold a security clearance.[32] If an Inspector determines that security issues are present, the Inspector consults the Associate Deputy Chief Inspector (ADCI) or the Deputy Chief Inspector (DCI). The ADCI normally oversees the investigation and approves the final report. Even though the DEA OPR management personnel are not as familiar with the *Adjudicative Guidelines* as are security personnel in OSP, they have the sole discretion to determine whether the allegation warrants referral to the OSP. If a referral is made, DEA OPR provides investigative support to OSP in its review of the matter.

In interviews, we learned that there is no formal process for referring misconduct allegations to OSP. Instead, the ADCI or the DCI merely discuss the allegations with OSP at their discretion. If the DEA OPR believes the case raises security issues, it provides OSP with access to the complete case file. Unless the misconduct allegation raises an immediate security concern, the referral does not occur until OPR completes the subject and witness interviews, or until the entire investigation is completed. DEA OPR officials explained that this is because of the potential that current investigations may be compromised if DEA OPR makes a referral to OSP while the subject or witnesses are still being interviewed. The DEA acknowledges that, historically, there

---

[31] This does not include four allegations where the subjects were DEA Task Force Officers (TFO) or the subjects retired while under inquiry. We did not include the TFO instances because the other components do not investigate TFO misconduct to the extent that DEA investigates these types of allegations. We also did not include eight allegations where a decision letter had not been issued as of this writing. Of the allegations that were included, one allegation involved a Country Attaché's improper sexual relationship with a drug trafficker's attorney, while the others involved two allegations where DEA agents and employees solicited prostitutes in the United States and overseas. The overseas prostitution case is discussed in detail in the text below.

[32] DEA *Office of Professional Responsibility Handbook*, undated.

have been no formal procedures for ensuring that the DEA OPR notifies the OSP of security clearance-related matters.

When referrals occur at the OPR's discretion, we found there is a risk that it may not identify misconduct allegations raising potential security concerns, which is neither the OPR's function nor its area of expertise. Below, we discuss a case in which several DEA employees working in an overseas office were alleged to have engaged in high-risk sexual behavior of a type that would be relevant under the Guidelines for determining their continued access to classified information, but where the ADCI or the DCI failed to refer the allegations to OSP.

Case Example: During a series of interviews the DEA OPR conducted from 2009 through 2010, former host-country police officers alleged that several DEA agents, consisting of an Assistant Regional Director (ARD), an Assistant Special Agent in Charge (ASAC), six Supervisory Special Agents (SSA), and two line Special Agents formerly assigned to the an overseas office, solicited prostitutes and engaged in other serious misconduct while in the country.[33]

The foreign officer allegedly arranged "sex parties" with prostitutes funded by the local drug cartels for these DEA agents at their government-leased quarters, over a period of several years. Although some of the DEA agents participating in these parties denied it, the information in the case file suggested they should have known the prostitutes in attendance were paid with cartel funds. A foreign officer also alleged providing protection for the DEA agents' weapons and property during the parties. The foreign officers further alleged that in addition to soliciting prostitutes, three DEA SSAs in particular were provided money, expensive gifts, and weapons from drug cartel members.

During the DEA OPR investigation, two DEA agents, who were subjects of the investigation, alleged that one of the SSAs frequented a

---

[33] The Assistant Regional Director (ARD) was not a subject of the subsequent investigation of the allegations by the DEA, but was instead deemed a witness. However, in interviews we learned that the DEA OPR Inspector assigned to the case had recommended the ARD be made a subject in light of allegations that the ARD solicited prostitutes at a farewell party held in the ARD's honor. DEA told the OIG that the Inspector's recommendation was considered and weighed against the evidence by the DEA OPR Senior Inspector, ADCI, and DCI, who all concluded that there was not enough evidence to justify disciplinary action against the ARD. The OIG believes that the parties who have the authority to determine whether there is sufficient evidence to warrant disciplinary action are the DEA HRB and HRO, not the DEA OPR. The ARD's failure to report other allegations that involved the solicitation of prostitutes and the DEA's failure to make the ARD a subject of this investigation are discussed in Chapter 1, the Reporting Process and Chapter 3, the Investigation Process.

prostitution establishment while in their overseas assignment and often took agents serving on temporary duty to this establishment and facilitated sexual encounters there. Another former foreign officer made similar allegations against the SSAs. Ultimately, 7 of the 10 agents admitted attending parties with prostitutes while they were stationed. The DEA imposed penalties ranging from a 2-day suspension to a 10-day suspension. One of the line agents was cleared of all wrongdoing.[34]

The DEA Inspector told us that prostitution is considered a part of the local culture and is tolerated in certain areas called "tolerance zones." According to the Inspector, it is common for prostitutes to be present at business meetings involving cartel members and foreign officers. The DEA Inspector also stated that the acceptability of this type of behavior affects the way in which federal law enforcement employees conduct themselves in this particular country. The Inspector further stated that prior to arriving in the country, agents needed better training that explicitly prohibits this type of conduct.[35]

DEA OPR did not refer this case to OSP to identify potential security risks for DEA and to assess the subjects' continued eligibility for a security clearance. In interviews, we learned that the assigned Inspector identified and discussed the potential security risks with OPR headquarters management. In particular, the Inspector said that she explained to OPR management that the fact that most of the "sex parties" occurred in government-leased quarters where agents' laptops, BlackBerry devices, and other government-issued equipment were

---

[34] We conducted multiple interviews with DEA officials regarding the manner in which these allegations were handled before the case was finally adjudicated. Despite evidence in the case file that many of the personnel we interviewed were involved with this investigation and adjudication, only one interviewee, the assigned DEA OPR Inspector, provided the OIG any meaningful information regarding this specific case in our initial interview. We learned about the involvement of the others from records we obtained after the matter was closed and, when we thereafter re-interviewed these individuals, they indicated that they believed that they were not supposed to provide information to us about pending matters. As noted previously, the OIG was entitled to this information at the outset, and the failure to provide it to us in a timely fashion unnecessarily delayed our review of this matter.

[35] The Inspector told us that, for example, in the wake of the Cartagena incident, the DEA instituted etiquette training also called "fork and knife" training for DEA employees who are permanently deployed overseas. However, the DEA did not initially provide this information to the OIG evaluators who examined the training the DEA and other components provide to federal employees who travel abroad (See U.S. Department of Justice Office of the Inspector General, *Review of Policies and Training Governing Off-Duty Conduct by Department Employees Working in Foreign Countries,* Report 15-2, January 2015).

present created potential security risks for the DEA and for the agents who participated in the parties, potentially exposing them to extortion, blackmail, or coercion.

Even though the Inspector said she discussed these risks with DEA OPR management, OPR management officials we interviewed said that they did not refer the allegations to OSP because OPR management did not believe that the special agents' conduct rose to the level of a security risk requiring a referral. It is also unclear whether the subjects self-reported these incidents, though if they did, there is no record of any review having been conducted by the OSP.[36] OSP officials told us they were not aware of this case and it was not referred to them.

We concluded that the alleged misconduct in this case clearly fell within the areas of concern identified in the *Adjudicative Guidelines* regarding continued access to classified information based on Sexual Behavior. Further, because prostitutes in the agents' quarters could easily have had access to sensitive DEA equipment and information, the misconduct also would be relevant to the concerns identified in the Adjudicative Guidelines on Foreign Influence, Personal Conduct, and Handling Protected Information Guidelines.[37] On both grounds, the absence of clear guidelines requiring the prompt reporting of this misconduct resulted in an ongoing security risk not being evaluated by the unit within the DEA assigned to that important duty. As a result of

---

[36] Department employees who have access to National Security Information (NSI), are in high-risk positions, or carry weapons in their official capacity are required to report in writing any on or off-duty allegations of misconduct to their respective Security Programs Manager. *See generally* Memo to Security Programs Managers, from James L. Dunlap, Department Security Officer, Justice Management Division, U.S. Department of Justice, *Self-Reporting of Arrests and Allegations of Misconduct,* September 10, 2004. In this case, we could not determine whether the subjects of the investigation self-reported the allegations discussed above.

[37] We found that some of the DEA Special Agents alleged to have solicited prostitutes were also involved in the investigations of the two former host country police officers who made these allegations. If these Special Agents had served as government witnesses at the trials of these defendants, their alleged misconduct would have had to be disclosed to defense attorneys and would likely have significantly impaired their ability to testify at trial. Ultimately, the government reached plea agreements with both defendants and the DEA Special Agents' misconduct did not prevent the government from achieving a favorable result in the narcotics conspiracy case. *See Giglio* v. *United States,* where the Supreme Court held that to ensure a fair trial, prosecutors must disclose material evidence that serves to impeach or undermine the credibility of government witnesses.

this review, the DEA has informed us that steps are being taken to improve the coordination between the DEA OPR and the DEA OSP.[38]

USMS

Of the 81 sexual misconduct and sexual harassment cases, we found 2 administratively closed cases involving high-risk sexual behavior where the Office of Internal Affairs failed to refer allegations to Office of Security Programs, Tactical Operations Division (OSP TOD) until well after the incidents occurred. These incidents may have presented potential security risks for the USMS and for the employees involved.[39] This occurred because the Office of Professional Responsibility, Internal Affairs (OPR-IA) lacks established written criteria for determining whether an allegation warrants a headquarters investigation or an investigation in the field and OPR-IA does not refer allegations that are investigated in the field to OSP TOD. The OPR-IA refers to OSP TOD only allegations investigated at headquarters, meaning that others sent back to the field are not referred to OSP TOD or reviewed there for potential security implications.

According to OPR-IA officials, the USMS employs a three-tier evaluation process to determine whether a case should be delegated to the originating office or fully investigated by headquarters Inspectors. The Deputy Chief Inspector, the Chief Inspector of OPR-IA, and the Deputy Assistant Director of the Office of Professional Responsibility review all allegations to determine where they will be investigated. Even though the USMS *Table of Offenses and Penalties* offers guidance on the range of penalties appropriate for certain types of misconduct, OPR-IA officials told us the reviewers do not consult it. Instead, they rely on their institutional knowledge and experience, choosing the cases they investigate without the benefit of written criteria. OPR-IA officials said

---

[38] The DEA informed the OIG that on May 5, 2014, an Inspection Division Coordination Committee was formed. An ongoing project of this committee is to formalize the process whereby DEA OPR makes timely notification to DEA OSP in instances when a security clearance issue is identified in a DEA OPR investigation. We were informed that on October 22, 2014, the committee made recommendations to address this issue but that no formal actions have been taken on any of the recommendations.

[39] The first case involved an employee's improper association with a criminal element. The case was monitored by the OIG. Specifically, it was alleged that a USMS employee's ex-wife was married to a suspected drug trafficker under DEA investigation. Although the USMS employee had dealings with the drug trafficker on numerous occasions, DEA and OIG found no evidence of criminal activity on the part of the USMS employee. The second case involved a Deputy U.S. Marshal (DUSM) who solicited prostitutes during an extradition mission overseas. This case is described in detail below.

that when the reviewers decide to refer an allegation back to the originating office in this matter, the OPR-IA does not refer the allegation to the OSP TOD.

One case of particular concern involved the solicitation of prostitutes overseas.

Case Example: According to the case file, in 2010, two Deputy U.S. Marshals (DUSMs) were assigned to conduct an extradition of a criminal defendant in Bangkok, Thailand. While in Thailand, one of the DUSMs was unavailable and, each time U.S. State Department officials attempted to contact him, two women with heavy foreign accents answered the phone and stated the DUSM could not be disturbed. A local investigator for the State Department spoke to one of the women in Thai, confirmed she was a prostitute, and instructed the DUSM's colleague to notify their management of the incident upon their return to the United States.

As instructed, the DUSM's colleague notified the supervisor about the incident. When the supervisor questioned the DUSM, the DUSM admitted having sexual relations with prostitutes while on the extradition mission. According to an e-mail in the case file, the supervisor orally admonished the DUSM and allegedly removed the DUSM from the list of Marshals permitted to go on extraditions. However, the USMS told us that there is no "extradition list" at USMS and assignments for extraditions are based on seniority in a DUSM's respective district. Since this incident, the DUSM has conducted at least one extradition overseas, even though the State Department stated in e-mail to the OIG that the DUSM was not welcome to return to Thailand.[40]

Based on our review of the case file, we determined that USMS Internal Affairs was not aware of the allegation until the State Department contacted the OIG directly to make a complaint, and the OIG subsequently referred the allegation back to USMS Internal Affairs for review since it did not involve an allegation of criminal conduct or administrative misconduct by a high-ranking component employee.[41]

---

[40] We were not able to determine which country the DUSM conducted extraditions in after this incident.

[41] The failure of the supervisor to report these allegations to USMS Internal Affairs is also discussed in Chapter 1. As discussed there, when we asked the supervisor why the allegation was not referred to USMS Internal Affairs, the supervisor asserted that supervisor did not believe the incident was misconduct, characterizing it instead as "a personal matter between him and his wife."

According to the case file, once the incident was reported to the OPR-IA, the Deputy Chief Inspector and the Chief Inspector decided to refer the matter back to the originating office for investigation, because such allegations would not warrant a suspension of 15 days or more. In addition, despite the DUSM's admissions to the supervisor, USMS officials told us this allegation was not investigated at headquarters because there was no evidence the DUSM had sex with prostitutes, and it was only the opinion of the State Department Deputy Regional Security Officer and a local investigator that the woman who answered the phone call was a prostitute. Further, in interviews with OPR-IA officials, we learned that there is no USMS policy prohibiting the solicitation of prostitutes in jurisdictions where prostitution is legal or tolerated.[42] As a result, according to these officials, the allegations would not warrant a suspension of 15 days or more and therefore did not require a headquarters investigation. Since a headquarters investigation did not occur, USMS security personnel were not notified about the misconduct.

Ultimately, the matter was closed at the originating office without an investigation and USMS security personnel were not informed about the incident until the subject's 5-year reinvestigation, nearly 2 years after the incident occurred. During the intervening years, the subject continued to hold a security clearance, with no review of the risks attendant to his behavior abroad.

However, USMS security personnel confirmed that the nature of this allegation and the involvement of the State Department constituted potential disqualifying behavior as described in *Adjudicative Guidelines on Sexual Behavior*. We learned that the OSP TOD required the DUSM to admit the conduct to the DUSM's spouse in order to mitigate potential security risks, such as potential exposure to coercion, extortion, and blackmail. Although the impact of the DUSM's conduct may have been mitigated in this manner, it took nearly 2 years after the incident to do so. Accordingly, the USMS was, at the very least, left open to potential security risks for longer than necessary.

This case exemplifies the need for better coordination between USMS Internal Affairs and the OSP TOD. All non-frivolous misconduct allegations involving USMS employees should be referred to OSP TOD, whether the allegation is investigated at headquarters or referred back to the originating office, to mitigate potential security risks when they are

---

[42] The OIG also examined the off-duty conduct policies that the USMS and other components provide to employees who travel abroad (See U.S. Department of Justice Office of the Inspector General, *Review of Policies and Training Governing Off-Duty Conduct by Department Employees Working in Foreign Countries,* Report 15-2, January 2015).

first discovered. Failing to do so presents security risks for USMS, hampers USMS's ability to determine an employee's continued eligibility to hold a security clearance, and has the potential to expose the employee involved to coercion, extortion, and blackmail for years, just as occurred in the case discussed above.

FBI

In contrast, the FBI has taken a better approach to addressing potential security issues. The FBI Internal Investigations Section refers all misconduct allegations to the Analysis and Investigations Unit (AIU). The AIU then determines whether the allegation raises security risks for the FBI or whether the allegation raises concerns about the employee's continued eligibility to hold a security clearance. If these risks are present, the AIU opens a parallel investigation. We consider the FBI's approach to be a best practice, and we believe ATF, the DEA, and the USMS should create a similar process. In the next chapter, we discuss issues that we discovered in the investigation of allegations of sexual misconduct and sexual harassment to headquarters.

CHAPTER 3: THE INVESTIGATION PROCESS

Components should have established criteria to determine whether an allegation is a management matter that can be handled locally or whether it warrants full investigation at headquarters. We found that ATF, DEA, and FBI have criteria regarding opening at their headquarters of investigations into allegations of sexual misconduct and sexual harassment. Although ATF generally followed established criteria for making such decisions, we found instances in which the FBI failed to follow its criteria and instances where the DEA failed to fully investigate allegations. USMS does not have established criteria, but generally seemed to make appropriate determinations about when to initiate an investigation in such matters.

DEA and FBI have established criteria to determine whether, after an allegation has been reported to headquarters, it should be investigated there or it can be referred back to be handled locally as a management matter. However, we found instances at DEA's Office of Professional Responsibility where it failed to fully investigate an allegation, or to even open an investigation on a particular subject, despite a recommendation from the assigned investigator.

At the FBI, we found instances where the Internal Investigations Section (IIS) at FBI headquarters did not open an investigation into allegations of sexual misconduct and sexual harassment, despite evidence in the case file reflecting that the subject had committed similar alleged misconduct in the past. In some instances, FBI's Internal Investigations Section referred such matters back to the field and recommended only counseling and sensitivity training.

The USMS does not have established criteria for determining whether an allegation should be handled locally or investigated at headquarters. Nevertheless, we generally found that the USMS made appropriate determinations about when to initiate an investigation at headquarters in such matters. Finally, we found that ATF generally followed its established criteria for determining whether an allegation should be handled locally or investigated at headquarters.

We describe our concerns about the DEA's and the FBI's practices in more detail below.

DEA

Generally, we found that the DEA OPR fully investigates all reported allegations of misconduct and does not refer matters back to local supervisors unless the matter reported is clearly a management or performance-related issue. This was true in 74 of the 77 cases (96 percent) we reviewed. We found that in 2 of the 77 cases the DEA OPR failed to fully investigate such cases, and we believe the DEA OPR closed the matters prematurely. While not great in number, we found these instances particularly troubling, and discuss them briefly below.

In related allegations involving the agents discussed in Case 1 of Chapter 1 above, the initial complaint alleged that a third agent also was involved in the solicitation of prostitutes. In an interview with the DEA OPR, the agent admitted traveling to the same overseas office on TDY approximately 20 times, to knowing both of the other subjects of the prostitution allegations, and to socializing with one of them. However, he denied soliciting prostitutes or knowing whether the other two SAs had solicited prostitutes.

Despite the third agent's admissions, it appears from our review of the file that the DEA OPR conducted only that one interview and then closed this case. When we asked the DEA OPR Inspector assigned why the case was closed without any additional investigation, the Inspector stated, "If you look a man in the eye and he answers no, then the answer is no - to do more is above my pay grade." We disagree and, at the very least, believe that the DEA OPR should have investigated further to determine the validity of these allegations, especially given the admissions regarding the agent's association with the other two SAs.

The second case involved an Assistant Regional Director (ARD) who allegedly solicited prostitutes at a farewell party held by the DEA overseas Country Office in the ARD's honor, and on other occasions. These allegations were made by a witness described in the DEA Case Example in Chapter 2, who recalled that six prostitutes were present at the farewell party, which took place in one of the agent's government-leased quarters. However, in his interview with DEA OPR, the ARD denied the allegations, stating that if anyone said he attended parties where prostitutes were present, they would be "100% lying."

Despite the DEA OPR Inspector's recommendation to include the ARD as a subject, the DEA OPR did not do so or, as far as we could tell, conduct any further investigation. Given the circumstances and the nature of the allegations, we believe the DEA OPR should have further investigated the allegations against the ARD, who was the highest ranking official alleged to have been involved with prostitutes.

Although the FBI has established criteria for determining whether an investigation should be opened at headquarters rather than being handled locally, we found that in 53 of 218 cases (24 percent) the FBI did not open headquarters investigations into allegations of sexual misconduct and sexual harassment, including 4 cases where the subject had reportedly committed such misconduct in the past. In 45 of these 53 cases (85 percent), the FBI closed the matter without further investigation, counseled the subject, or the subject was disciplined on other charges. In 8 of the 53 cases (15 percent), the allegations appeared to fall within Offense Code 5.20, Sexual Harassment, requiring a headquarters investigation, but FBI failed to conduct one and instead referred the matters back to the field and recommended counseling and training.

In interviews, we learned that the FBI Internal Investigations Section relies on the FBI offense table and staff experience to determine whether an allegation should be investigated at headquarters, referred back to the field for investigation, or closed. The FBI offense table also contains designations in certain offense categories where the investigation can be delegated to the field, and there are no offense categories of a sexual nature in the FBI offense table that allow for a field investigation. Nevertheless, we found instances in which serious sexual misconduct allegations were referred back to the field. We discuss two cases below.

Case #1: According to case file we reviewed, on at least four occasions, a Management and Program Analyst (MAPA) was alleged to have made inappropriate comments of a graphic sexual nature to a contract employee, which included comments about the contractor's "anatomical body parts and breasts." The contractor was too embarrassed to repeat the specific comments, but another employee who witnessed the alleged misconduct reported it to division management. The contract employee also alleged that the MAPA made inappropriate comments, not of a sexual nature, that she perceived as demeaning to other female employees.

Even though division management had counseled the MAPA in the past for making demeaning comments to other employees, the IIS declined to open an investigation. Instead, the IIS relied upon division management to counsel the MAPA about the comments. During the counseling, the MAPA stated that the comments were "jokes" between friends and were not meant to be disturbing or offensive. The Unit Chief documented the counseling and provided a written record to the MAPA so he was clear as to what was discussed. The Unit Chief also changed the MAPA's hours of work, closely supervised the MAPA, and sent the MAPA to interpersonal skills training. The IIS was satisfied with the division management's handling of the alleged misconduct and advised the division to monitor the situation and report any further incidents to headquarters.

We note that the Department has a zero tolerance policy on harassment in the workplace.[43] In this particular matter, division management appeared to treat the alleged conduct seriously by taking some corrective action; but we nevertheless found these allegations should have been fully investigated at headquarters because the comments made about the contractor appear to fall within the *Sexual Misconduct – Non Consensual* offense category. Based on the FBI offense table, this offense category warrants a headquarters investigation and cannot be handled solely in the field. The Unit Chief's description of the misconduct as "sexually harassing" when reporting the allegations to IIS and the fact that the penalty range of Sexual Misconduct – Non-Consensual does not include counseling provides additional support for ensuring that the matter was investigated at FBI headquarters rather than handled in the field.

Case #2: An anonymous complaint alleged that a Supervisory Intelligence Analyst (IA) allegedly made unwanted sexual advances and remarks to several female employees in five specified instances. One of the female employees alleged that the subject followed her around the office until she discovered the subject was doing so. Upon being the discovered, the subject pretended that he had gotten lost, despite having worked in office for 2 years. In another incident, the subject reportedly made romantically suggestive remarks toward a female employee after learning that she was single. The subject then initiated a hug with the employee and touched their cheeks together. The female employees were not identified in the complaint. Even though the IIS had received three other complaints against the subject about other alleged misconduct, the IIS declined to investigate the allegations and instead recommended that the field division counsel the subject.[44]

A few months after the first complaint, the IIS received a second anonymous complaint alleging that the same subject had made an inappropriate comment to a new IA in the division. The complainant

---

[43] See http://ww.justice.gov/jmd/eeos/agmemo.html

[44] This case was not originally provided by the FBI in response to our data and document request, and was determined to be within the scope of our review with the assistance of the OIG Investigations Division.

alleged that the subject stated to her, "If I was not married, I would be all about you." She further alleged that the subject "preys on young females that are fairly new to the Bureau and knows they are too afraid to report his comments." The IIS again determined the allegations did not warrant a full investigation at headquarters, and instead recommended that division management treat the matter as a performance issue and counsel the subject again. In a written comment on the allegation summary, an IIS official noted, "It is obvious someone does not like [the subject]."

Given the repeated nature and substance of the comments the subject allegedly made, we believe that the alleged misconduct falls squarely within Offense Code 5.20, Sexual Harassment, which includes unwanted sexual advances. Since field investigations are not permitted for this offense category, we found that the FBI IIS should have opened a headquarters investigation as required by FBI policy.

In the next chapter of this report, we discuss issues that we discovered in the adjudication process.

CHAPTER 4: THE ADJUDICATION PROCESS

Our review of the law enforcement offense tables found that the FBI, DEA, and USMS offense tables contain specific offense categories to address allegations of sexual misconduct and sexual harassment and to provide guidance on the appropriate range of penalties that could be imposed.[45] However, we determined that for some offense categories, the DEA and USMS offense tables do not provide adequate explanations of the types of behaviors that warrant possible disciplinary action. Further, we found that these components applied general offense categories to misconduct we believe is more appropriately addressed by the specific sexual harassment and sexual misconduct offense categories contained in their offense tables.

The ATF offense table does not contain specific offense categories to address sexual misconduct and sexual harassment. Instead, the offense table contains general descriptions of the types of misconduct that could be charged under various offense categories with a broad range of possible penalties.[46]

While the FBI offense table contains specific language to address the solicitation of prostitutes overseas even where the conduct is legal or tolerated, we found that the ATF, DEA, and USMS offense tables do not contain specific language to address this form of misconduct.[47] As a result, the employees of these components may not know whether it is prohibited and may not have adequate notice of the range of penalties that could be imposed.

See Appendix 3 for detailed information on the types of offense categories used by the law enforcement components to address sexual misconduct and sexual harassment.

---

[45] During adjudication, an adjudicative case file contains only information relating to an individual subject. Therefore, when discussing the adjudicative process, we refer to each subject as a case. Note that "case" in this chapter carries a different meaning than in other sections of the report.

[46] ATF, the DEA, and the FBI use "activity codes" that more accurately reflect the type of alleged misconduct committed by an employee. Presumably, these codes could be used to determine the nature and frequency of alleged sexual misconduct and sexual harassment. However, the activity codes are assigned to an allegation at the beginning of the investigation and may not reflect the allegations that were substantiated at the close of the investigation.

[47] See U.S. Department of Justice Office of the Inspector General, *Review of Policies and Training Governing Off-Duty Conduct by Department Employees Working in Foreign Countries,* Report 15-2, January 2015.

The ATF Guide for Offenses and Penalties (the Guide or ATF offense table) is used to provide guidance concerning the types of discipline that may result when an employee commits misconduct. The Guide is divided into 11 sections.[48] Despite the extensive number of offense categories, the Guide does not contain any specific category designed to address sexual misconduct allegations. The ATF offense table contains an offense category directed at supervisors for failing to report allegations of sexual harassment, but it does not address the underlying misconduct directly. Moreover, this offense category does not define sexual harassment, and it is not specifically defined anywhere in the table.

Based on the explanations provided in the Guide, there are a number of general offense categories where sexual misconduct could be charged. For example, under the offense category, *Poor Judgment and/or Conduct Unbecoming a Federal Employee/Special Agent,* the explanation describes, "engaging in sexual activity in an ATF office space or government vehicle" as conduct that may warrant a charge under this offense category.

In the explanation for the offense category *Inappropriate Behavior,* the Guide states that an ATF employee who is "inappropriate toward co-workers, subordinates, or supervisors by teasing, jokes, gestures, or display of materials of a sexual nature, or an employee who makes sexual remarks" may be charged under this offense category. Given the explanation contained in this offense category, misconduct equivalent to sexual harassment could be charged under this offense category. Finally, the explanation for the offense category *Association with Disreputable Persons* describes "improper personal relationships with convicted felons, informants and subjects of investigations" as conduct they may be charged under this offense category. We describe ATF's use of the offense categories below:

- In 6 of the 12 (50 percent) adjudicated sexual misconduct cases, the ATF Deciding Official charged employees under the *Poor Judgment and/or Conduct Unbecoming* offense category. The cases involved 1 improper association with a criminal

---

[48] The 11 sections in the ATF Guide for Offenses and Penalties are: (1) government property and resources, (2) government-owned vehicles, (3) ATF-issued firearms, (4) improper use of force/weapons, (5) general integrity related misconduct, (6) drugs and alcohol, (7) falsification, (8) misconduct connected to performance of duties, (9) attendance, (10) improper handling of evidence or property taken into bureau custody, and (11) security.

element case, 3 "sexting" cases, 1 case involving solicitation of prostitutes, and the case we discussed in Chapter 2 involving solicitation of multiple consensual sex partners while on official travel.[49]

- In three cases, the subjects were charged with *Misuse of their Government Vehicle* to facilitate an intimate or sexual relationship. In two of these three cases, the subjects had also committed multiple offenses (inappropriate relationship with a subordinate in one case and lack of candor, falsification of government documents, and misuse of government property in the other case) and were charged accordingly.

- The remaining three cases related to sexual harassment. Two of the subjects committed misconduct described as a violation of ATF Order 1050.5, *Prevention and Elimination of Sexual Harassment in the Workplace*. However, as we noted above, this offense category is not discussed in the ATF offense table as a separate category. In one case the subject was removed from service, while in another case the subject received a letter of caution.[50] The three subjects were not charged under the *Inappropriate Behavior* offense category, which contains explanatory language in the offense table that describes misconduct that is comparable to sexual harassment.

Although the unofficial offense category based on the ATF Order captures the type of misconduct committed, the subject employees would not have notice of the range of penalties because it is not included in the ATF offense table.

In interviews, ATF officials acknowledged that there are no specific offense categories in the ATF offense table to address sexual misconduct and sexual harassment. According to these officials, the ATF Professional Review Board and the ATF Deciding Official generally charge employees who commit this type of misconduct using the *Poor Judgment* and *Conduct Unbecoming a Federal Employee/Special Agent* offense categories.

ATF officials also commented that this type of misconduct has not been an area of concern because it appears to occur infrequently.

---

[49] Based on the substantiated allegations described in the case file, the subject could have been charged with *Association with Disreputable Persons*.

[50] For the ATF employee who was removed from service, ATF has no additional information that the employee appealed the decision through the MSPB.

However, ATF officials said that they recognized the deficiencies in their offense table as compared to the other law enforcement components. We were told that in early 2013 ATF constituted a working group to revise the offense table to include new offense categories to address sexual misconduct and sexual harassment. On January 29, 2015, we were told that the ATF Guide to Offenses and Penalties had been updated on October 1, 2014; however, no new offense for sexual misconduct and sexual harassment was included because ATF believes that the existing charges already address those matters. In addition, ATF informed the OIG that the working group will be reviewing the ATF Guide for Offenses and Penalties on an annual basis.

In interviews, we learned that the offense table is included in the *Integrity Bulletins* provided to employees. However, because the offense tables do not contain specific language regarding prohibited behavior, ATF employees may not know what types of conduct are prohibited and may not have adequate notice of the range of penalties that could be imposed. In addition, there is also a risk that inconsistent penalties could be imposed for similar misconduct based upon vagaries in classification. Further, it may be difficult for ATF to easily determine the frequency of this type of misconduct or any trends in the types of allegations reported that might be helpful in assessing the need for further guidance and training.

DEA

The DEA Guide of Disciplinary Offenses and Penalties (the DEA Guide or DEA offense table) is divided into 11 sections and is the offense table DEA uses to provide guidance concerning the types of discipline that may result when an employee commits misconduct.[51] There are seven offense categories in the DEA offense table summarized in Appendix 3 that could address allegations of sexual misconduct and sexual harassment. Four of the seven categories are specifically designed to address such behavior. The DEA Guide describes the offense category *Unprofessional or Inappropriate Conduct of a Sexual Nature* as "teasing, jokes, actions, gestures, display of materials or remarks of a sexual nature." The penalty for this offense ranges from reprimand to removal.

---

[51] The 11 sections in the DEA Guide of Disciplinary Offenses and Penalties are: (1) attendance issues, (2) fiscal issues, (3) false statements or incorrect official documents, (4) harassment/discrimination, (5) law enforcement specific offenses, (6) failure to follow, (7) negligent work, (8) health and safety issues, (9) security issues, (10) supervisory misconduct, and (11) conduct prejudicial to the DEA and the Department.

The DEA Guide cites Title VII of the *Civil Rights Act of 1964* when defining the *Sexual Harassment* offense category in the offense table, which also contains an offense category for "Retaliation against an employee resulting from or in connection with an allegation of sexual harassment." However, the only penalty suggested for both of these violations is removal.

The DEA Guide also contains other offense categories that do not specifically address sexual misconduct but may, under certain circumstances, be considered sexual misconduct, including *Improper Association with a Convicted Felon, Confidential Source and/or Persons Connected with Criminal Activity, Disrespectful or Unprofessional Conduct, Conduct Unbecoming a DEA Employee,* and *Criminal, Dishonest and Notoriously Disgraceful Conduct.* The categories *Conduct Unbecoming a DEA Employee* and *Criminal, Dishonest and Notoriously Disgraceful Conduct* are not defined in the offense table.

We found that even though two DEA offense categories are specifically designed to address allegations of sexual misconduct and sexual harassment, no DEA employees with substantiated allegations were charged under either of them. Instead, in 20 of 33 (61 percent) adjudicated cases, the employees were charged under the general offense categories. Where the subject committed multiple offenses, they were charged under additional offense categories based on the facts of the case. We describe the DEA's use of the offense categories below:

- In 10 adjudicated cases we reviewed, the alleged misconduct appeared to involve allegations of sexual harassment, yet none of the subjects were charged under that offense category. Instead, they were charged with *Conduct Unbecoming DEA Agent/Non-Agent* exclusively, or with both *Conduct Unbecoming* and *Failure to Follow Written Instructions.*

In interviews, a DEA disciplinary official said that he is reluctant to charge an employee with sexual harassment because he believes most DEA employees do not commit sexual harassment that would rise to the level of a Title VII violation, for which the only penalty under the offense table is removal. When we asked why the *Sexual Harassment* offense category is in the offense table if DEA officials do not use it, one DEA official who is heavily involved in the discipline process responded, "It's for show."

- In seven adjudicated cases we reviewed, the alleged misconduct appeared to involve the solicitation of prostitutes, both domestically and overseas, but none of the subjects were charged under *Criminal, Dishonest or Notoriously Disgraceful*

Conduct, a category that other government agencies use to address this form of misconduct. Instead, they were charged with *Conduct Unbecoming a DEA Employee, Poor Judgment,* or were charged under both of these offense categories. However, we determined that there is no *Poor Judgment* offense category in the DEA Guide. Therefore, some DEA employees are being charged inconsistently, which raises a potential that employees may receive inconsistent penalties for similar misconduct.

- In three adjudicated cases we examined, the alleged misconduct involved multiple offenses, including an inappropriate relationship between a supervisor and subordinate, an inappropriate relationship between a DEA employee and a vendor, improper association with a criminal element, and covertly videotaping a naked female. These cases could have been charged under *Unprofessional or Inappropriate Conduct of a Sexual Nature* or *Improper Association with a Convicted Felon* rather than *Conduct Unbecoming* and *Poor Judgment.* As a result, some DEA employees are being charged inconsistently for similar conduct because proposing/deciding officials have greater discretion when imposing discipline under these catch-all offense categories.

By contrast, in the remaining 13 adjudicated cases we reviewed, DEA officials appear to have charged the subject under the most applicable offense category. In one case, the alleged misconduct involved an improper association with a confidential informant (sexual relationship) and making false statements and the subject was charged under those respective offense categories. The remaining 12 cases involved the transmission of sexually explicit e-mail, text messages, and images. Those cases were charged under *Misuse of Government Property.*

In interviews, DEA officials explained that they are afforded wide latitude when making discipline decisions under the *Conduct Unbecoming a DEA Employee* offense category, which supports penalties ranging from a letter of reprimand to removal. When we asked why DEA officials do not charge under the *Criminal, Dishonest or Notoriously Disgraceful Conduct* or *Inappropriate Conduct of a Sexual Nature* offense categories where the subject had solicited prostitutes, one DEA official told us that *Conduct Unbecoming* or *Poor Judgment* has always been charged in cases of this type. The DEA official also stated that the *Criminal, Dishonest or Notoriously Disgraceful Conduct* offense category offers less flexibility to proposing and deciding officials, with penalties ranging from suspension of 14 days to removal. He said that therefore, DEA officials have traditionally not used it. However, our review of the

DEA Guide showed *Unprofessional or Inappropriate Conduct of a Sexual Nature* contains the same penalty range as *Conduct Unbecoming.*

This DEA official also told us that DEA officials have not charged employees with a penalty greater than a suspension of 14 days (a suspension of greater than 14 days would be considered an adverse action) in prior cases involving the solicitation of prostitutes where the conduct was legal or tolerated in the jurisdiction. He said that therefore it would not be appropriate to charge a DEA employee under the *Criminal, Dishonest or Notoriously Disgraceful Conduct* offense category in such circumstances.

We found that DEA has two specific offense categories, *Sexual Harassment* and *Unprofessional or Inappropriate Conduct of a Sexual Nature*, that are adequate to address allegations of sexual misconduct and sexual harassment, and yet we observed that DEA officials overwhelmingly charge employees under the most general offense category in their guide, *Conduct Unbecoming a DEA Employee.* Since the only penalty listed under the *Sexual Harassment* offense category is removal, it is understandable why officials may be reluctant to lose all flexibility in addressing situations where the circumstances and any mitigating factors may vary significantly.

DEA might consider amending the penalties for this offense category to provide somewhat greater flexibility along the lines of the identical category in the USMS offense table, though that has not resulted in greater use of the category as discussed below. Moreover, the offense category *Unprofessional or Inappropriate Conduct of a Sexual Nature* has a range of penalties from letter of reprimand to removal, and we believe that this offense category could be properly charged in a variety of situations where the alleged conduct was sexual in nature.

In addition, we found that DEA officials have unofficially created the *Poor Judgment* offense category, which is not included in the offense table. The use of an offense category not listed in the table is of particular concern because there is no explanation for when it may be applied or what range of penalties may be imposed. By disregarding the DEA Guide and using this offense category, proposing and deciding officials are provided more discretion than what the offense table already provides. The only limit to this discretion is the requirement that proposing and deciding officials must consult prior cases when rendering disciplinary decisions.

When DEA officials use general offense categories to make disciplinary decisions, DEA employees may not know what types of conduct are prohibited and may not have adequate notice of the range of penalties that could be imposed. There is also a risk that inconsistent penalties could be imposed for similar misconduct.

Further, it may be difficult for DEA to easily determine the frequency of this type of misconduct or any trends in the types of allegations reported. In fact, when we initially requested case information regarding misconduct allegations of this type for our review, DEA officials repeatedly told us how difficult it would be for them to determine the number of allegations that occurred during our study period. These DEA officials cited DEA investigators' and adjudicators' use of general offense categories as one of the reasons that the OIG's request presented challenges.

FBI

The FBI Offense Table and Penalty Guidelines (the Guidelines) outline a range of penalties applicable to various types of employee misconduct. Of the law enforcement components, the FBI offense table has the greatest number of offense categories that could apply to sexual harassment and sexual misconduct. The Guidelines divide offenses into five sections, with five general and six specific offense categories designed to address this form of misconduct.[52] The general offense categories include *Disruptive Behavior, Other Felonies, Other Misdemeanors,* and *Unprofessional Conduct On and Off Duty.* See Appendix 3 for more detailed information about these offense categories.

The specific offense categories contained in the table include *Asset/CW/Informant/CHS (Source) – Improper Personal Relationship, Indecent/Lascivious Acts, Improper Relationship – Superior/Subordinate, Improper Relationship with a Criminal Element,* and *Sexual Harassment* and *Sexual Misconduct – Consensual.*

Although we found that the FBI offense table has six specific offense categories that could adequately address sexual misconduct and sexual harassment, we also found that in some cases general offense categories were used. We describe the FBI's use of the offense categories below:

- In 41 of the 102 (40 percent) adjudicated sexual misconduct and sexual harassment cases, FBI officials charged employees under the *Unprofessional Conduct – Off Duty* and *Unprofessional Conduct – On Duty* offense categories. In 14 of the 41 cases, the

---

[52] The FBI Offense Table and Penalty Guidelines is divided into five sections including: (1) investigative misconduct, (2) integrity/ethical misconduct, (3) property related misconduct, (4) illegal/criminal conduct, and (5) general misconduct.

FBI offense table contained specific offense categories that we believe more specifically reflected the conduct committed.

- In 4 of the 16 of the adjudicated cases involving alleged sexual harassment, inappropriate touching and/or groping, the subjects were charged under the unprofessional conduct offense categories rather than *Sexual Harassment* or *Sexual Misconduct – Non-Consensual* offense categories.

- Despite having a clear offense category in the FBI offense table designed to address inappropriate personal relationships with confidential sources, witnesses, and informants, FBI officials charged 2 of the 5 subjects who committed this offense under the unprofessional conduct offense categories. In 6 of the 11 adjudicated cases involving the solicitation of prostitutes, the subjects were charged under the unprofessional conduct offense categories rather than under the *Indecent/Lascivious Acts* offense category.

In one of the six cases, where the subject was charged with *Unprofessional Conduct – Off Duty* rather than *Indecent/Lascivious Acts,* we found this decision particularly troubling given that the subject, a former Assistant Section Chief responsible for training agents and others abroad on child exploitation and human trafficking issues, had engaged in multiple consensual and commercial sexual encounters over a 7-year period with foreign nationals, including prostitutes, strippers, students in his classes, and members of foreign law enforcement. In addition, false and misleading reports the subject made after his conduct was discovered would have warranted charging him under the *Lack of Candor* and *False/Misleading Information – Employment/Security Document.*

Despite this troubling case, we found that of the four law enforcement components, the FBI's offense table can serve as a model for the other components in that it clearly addresses allegations of sexual misconduct and sexual harassment. According to the FBI offense table, the *Unprofessional Conduct* offense categories were fashioned to aid deciding officials in rendering decisions when there was no other specific offense category adequate to address the misconduct committed. However, when FBI or other officials disregard the specific offense categories in the offense table, the only check on their discretion is the requirement that proposing and deciding officials consult case precedent when making disciplinary decisions. Therefore, charging employees under general offense categories could result in the imposition of inconsistent penalties. Further, when charging officials disregard the offense table in this manner, FBI employees may not have full notice regarding the types of conduct that are prohibited and the range of penalties that could be imposed.

In addition, charging employees under general offense categories may prevent the FBI from being able to determine the overall number of reported sexual misconduct and sexual harassment cases. When we initially requested case information on misconduct allegations of this type, FBI officials repeatedly explained how difficult it would be to determine the number of allegations that occurred during the study period. The FBI officials cited the adjudicators' use of general offense categories as one of the reasons why the OIG's request presented challenges.

USMS

The USMS Guidance Table of Disciplinary Offenses and Penalties (the Guide) is divided into 11 sections and is virtually identical to the DEA Guide for Disciplinary Offenses and Penalties.[53]

Similar to the DEA Guide, there are eight offense categories that could be used to address allegations of sexual misconduct. Three of the eight categories are specifically designed to address it. The Guide describes the offense category *Unprofessional or Inappropriate Conduct of a Sexual Nature* as "teasing, jokes, actions, gestures, display of materials or remarks of a sexual nature." The penalty for this offense ranges from reprimand to removal.

The Guide cites Title VII of the *Civil Rights Act of 1964* when defining the sexual harassment offense category, and it contains another offense category, *Retaliation against an Employee Resulting from or in Connection with an Allegation of Sexual Harassment.* Unlike the DEA Guide, the penalty for sexual harassment at USMS ranges from a 5-day suspension to removal. The penalty for retaliation resulting from an allegation of sexual harassment ranges from reprimand to removal.

We determined that the Guide also contains other offense categories that do not specifically address sexual misconduct, but may, under certain circumstances, be considered sexual misconduct, including *Improper Association with a Convicted Felon or Witness Protection Program Participant, Confidential Source and/or Persons Connected with Criminal Activity, Conduct Unbecoming a USMS Employee,*

---

[53] The Guide has 11 sections: (1) attendance issues, (2) fiscal issues, (3) false statements or incorrect official documents, (4) harassment/discrimination, (5) law enforcement specific offenses, (6) failure to follow, (7) negligent work, (8) health and safety issues, (9) security issues, (10) supervisory misconduct, and (11) conduct prejudicial to USMS and the Department.

Criminal, Dishonest and Notoriously Disgraceful Conduct, Disrespectful or Unprofessional Conduct, and *Off-duty Misconduct.* We noted that the USMS Guide does not specifically define *Criminal, Dishonest and Notoriously Disgraceful Conduct, Conduct Unbecoming a USMS employee,* and *Off-duty Misconduct* in the table.

We found that even though two USMS offense categories are specifically designed to address allegations of sexual misconduct and sexual harassment, no USMS employees with substantiated allegations were charged under either of them. Instead, in 21 of 32 (66 percent) adjudicated cases, the USMS officials charged employees under the general offense categories. Where the subject committed multiple offenses, they were charged under additional offense categories based on the facts of the case. We discuss USMS's use of the offense categories below:

- In the only two adjudicated cases where the alleged misconduct appeared to involve allegations of sexual harassment, none of the subjects were charged under that offense category. Instead, they were charged with *Conduct Unbecoming a USMS employee* exclusively or *Conduct Unbecoming* and other offense categories based on the facts of the case.

In interviews, USMS deciding officials told us that in the prior cases they review before making decisions, adjudicators had charged general offense categories. The officials told us that they had followed the decisions of their predecessors.

- In three of the six adjudicated cases where the alleged misconduct involved the transmission of sexually explicit e-mail, text messages, and images, the subjects were charged with *Conduct Unbecoming* rather than *Misuse of Internet and/or Unauthorized Use of Federal Telecommunication System, Commercial Long Distance.*

- In five of the seven adjudicated cases where the alleged misconduct involved inappropriate relationships, the subjects were charged with *Conduct Unbecoming, Violation of the Rules of Professional Responsibility,* and *Displaying Poor Judgment* rather than *Unprofessional or Inappropriate Conduct of a Sexual Nature.* Similarly to DEA, *Displaying Poor Judgment* is not an offense category in the USMS offense table.

- In all seven of the adjudicated cases where the alleged misconduct involved the subjects making inappropriate comments or gestures of a sexual nature, the subjects were charged with *Conduct Unbecoming* and *Disrespectful Conduct* rather than *Unprofessional or Inappropriate Conduct of a Sexual Nature.* In one of these cases, no charge was specified in the letter of reprimand issued.

- In two of the six adjudicated cases that involved a USMS employee having an inappropriate relationship with a criminal element, the subjects were charged with *Conduct Unbecoming, Displaying Poor Judgment,* or they were charged under both offense categories. As previously noted, *Displaying Poor Judgment* is not an offense category in the USMS offense table. One of the subjects was also charged under other specific offense categories based on the facts of the case.

- In two cases, the subjects were charged with *Conduct Unbecoming* rather than *Unprofessional or Inappropriate Conduct of a Sexual Nature* or *Misuse of Government Property.* In one case, one DUSM and a courtroom clerk had sexual relations after hours in a courtroom, while in the other case the subject had sexual relations in USMS office space.

By contrast, we found that in 11 of the 32 adjudicated cases involving the transmission of sexually explicit e-mail, text messages, and images; misuse of a government vehicle; improper associations with criminal elements; and inappropriate relationships, the subjects were charged under the more specific offense categories.

We believe that charging USMS employees under general offense categories may result in USMS employees not having full notice as to what types of conduct are prohibited and the range of penalties that could be imposed. Further, the use of general offense categories by deciding officials may result in the imposition of inconsistent penalties and may prevent the USMS from being able to determine the overall number of sexual misconduct and sexual harassment cases.

We also found that USMS officials created the *Displaying Poor Judgment* offense category, a category that is not included in the offense table. By disregarding the USMS Guide and using this offense category, proposing and deciding officials have more discretion than what is provided in the offense table.

In the final chapter, we will discuss other issues we identified during our review of sexual misconduct and sexual harassment allegations.

CHAPTER 5: DETECTING AND RETAINING SEXUALLY EXPLICIT TEXT MESSAGE EVIDENCE

According to a 2013 research study conducted by the Pew Research Center's Internet and American Life Project, 91 percent of American adults own cell phones and more than three-quarters of them (81 percent) send and receive text messages.[54] Therefore, it is no surprise law enforcement employees with government-issued mobile devices use this convenient and useful technology in their day-to-day business communications. However, some employees abuse this privilege and send sexually explicit text messages, images, and e-mails on their government-issued devices and computers. We found that all the components have weaknesses in detecting and tracking the transmission of sexually explicit text messages, also known as "sexting." We also found that ATF, the DEA, and the USMS have weaknesses in detecting and tracking the transmission of sexually explicit images. Therefore, we were unable to determine the actual number of instances involving this type of misconduct. Despite not being able to determine the actual number, we found that sexting was the second most commonly alleged offense in the cases we examined.[55]

We found that the FBI and USMS archive text messages sent and received by employees on their government-issued devices, so that they are available for investigators and as evidence in subsequent legal proceedings. However, the FBI is hampered in its ability to archive all text messages sent and received by its employees due to technological limitations. The FBI proactively monitors the text messages its employees receive but relies on third parties to provide text message data. Further, the FBI has disabled the ability to send images on employee BlackBerry devices. By contrast, the USMS does not proactively monitor text messages sent by its employees, despite its ability to do so, and cannot detect the transmission of sexually explicit photographs or images.

We found that ATF and DEA are unable to archive the text messages of their employees and are generally unable to detect this form of misconduct. Further, misconduct investigators at ATF, the DEA, and the USMS cannot easily obtain text messages that may be important evidence in their investigations. In some instances, these components relied on the employees involved in the investigations to provide this

---

[54] Maeve Duggan, Pew Research Center's Internet and American Life Project, *Cell Phone Activities 2013*, September 16, 2013.

[55] See Appendix 4 for additional information about this category of sexual misconduct.

evidence. This is problematic because the employees providing the evidence may adulterate it or not provide complete evidence to the investigators. There is also a risk these components may be hampered in their ability to fulfill their discovery obligations.

Discovery Obligations and Text Message Evidence

The Department policies related to the disclosure of exculpatory and impeachment evidence, *Disclosure of Exculpatory and Impeachment Information* (*Brady* Policy), and *Potential Impeachment Information Concerning Law Enforcement Witnesses* (*Giglio* Policy), are set forth in the United States Attorneys' Manual (USAM) at Sections 9-5.001 and 9-5.100, respectively.[56] A March 2011 memo from the Deputy Attorney General directed the leadership of the Department law enforcement components and the litigating divisions to ensure that all prosecution and law enforcement personnel participating as members of a "prosecution team" preserve "e-communications," defined to include "e-mails, text messages, SMS (short message), instant messages (IM), voice mail, pin-to-pin communications [Personal Identification Number (PIN)], social networking sites, bulletin boards, blogs, and similar means of electronic communication," as these e-communications may be discoverable prior to trial.[57]

The guidance instructs members of the prosecution team to think about the content of any e-communication before sending it, ensure appropriate language is used, and determine in advance how to preserve potentially discoverable information. In addition, the guidance also recognized the unique challenges the components may face when attempting to produce (text, SMS, IM, PIN) evidence. The guidance instructs the components to provide guidance to employees on how to preserve this type of evidence and directs the components to document any inability to do so that it can be explained in court.

---

[56] *See generally Brady* v. *Maryland*, 373 U.S. 83 (1963), and *Giglio* v. *United States*, 405 U.S. 150 (1972).

[57] *See generally* Memo to the Associate Attorney General and the Assistant Attorneys General for the Criminal Division, National Security Division, Civil Rights Division, Antitrust Division, Environment and Natural Resources Division, the Tax Division, the Directors of FBI, DEA, USMS, ATF, and the BOP, and all United States Attorneys from Deputy Attorney General, James M. Cole, *Guidance on the Use, Preservation, and Disclosure of Electronic Communications in Federal Criminal Cases,* March 30, 2011. The "prosecution team" for this purpose includes federal, state, and local law enforcement officers and other government officials participating in the investigation and prosecution of the criminal case against the defendant. USAM 9-5.001.

In relation to e-communications, there are a variety of circumstances in which such communications may constitute or contain discoverable material under these standards.[58] For example, e-communications may indicate a possible relationship, intimate or otherwise, between a member of the prosecution team and a victim, cooperating witness, informant, or other source of information that may serve as bias or improper motive evidence or otherwise be a subject for impeachment of the government witness.[59]

Law Enforcement Witnesses and *Brady/Giglio* Issues

Although Agency Officials at some of the components review e-mail messages for possible *Brady/Giglio* issues, Agency Officials at ATF and the DEA told us that they do not review text messages for these issues because they lack the technology to archive such material. Instead, they said they rely on the law enforcement witnesses at these components to provide prosecutors with what they deem to be relevant text messages.[60] By allowing law enforcement witnesses to independently determine what text message evidence is subject to discovery under *Brady* or *Giglio*, without further oversight or review, there is a risk that witnesses may not provide all relevant text messages or may adulterate the text messages before providing them. In addition, under the Department's *Giglio* Policy, Agency Officials should consult with prosecutors assigned to the cases to determine whether case law or court rulings in the district require broader disclosures to ensure that all potentially discoverable material is disclosed.

The Deputy Attorney General's March 2011 memo warned the components that the preservation of certain messaging formats including text, SMS, instant, and PIN presented unique challenges and posed risks for the Department's cases if these messaging formats were not

---

[58] Although our primary discussion centers on *Brady/Giglio* obligations, this issue may also arise in discovery during civil cases. For example, if someone sues for sexual harassment, the component might be obligated to produce text message evidence during discovery.

[59] *See generally United States* v. *W.R. Grace*, 401 F. Supp. 2d 1069 (D. Mont., 2005), where the government's main cooperating witness exchanged roughly 200 e-mails with the lead case agent over a 4-year period leading up to trial. The defense did not learn about these e-mails until partway through the cooperating witness's cross examination. The court determined the e-mails showed significant bias in the form of the cooperator's extensive relationship with the government agents and animus toward the defendant, and instructed the jury to that effect.

[60] It is ATF and DEA policy that all substantive case-related text messages be preserved and potentially be made available during discovery.

preserved. In an interview with an Office of the Deputy Attorney General (ODAG) official, we learned that these challenges have confronted the law enforcement components for several years and are yet to be fully resolved.

For years, federal judges have required companies to implement costly litigation holds covering offices worldwide to preserve potentially discoverable text messages in civil and criminal cases.[61] After unfavorable court rulings, ODAG officials recognized the importance of this issue and constituted a working group to address it. According to ODAG officials we interviewed, the working group included representatives from ATF, the DEA, and the FBI.[62] During discussions over the last 3 years, ODAG officials said they cautioned the components about the risks associated with not establishing a system for archiving text messages in the same manner e-mail messages are archived on their backup servers.

At the working group meetings, both ATF and DEA told ODAG officials that they are unable to archive the text messages of their employees because the operating systems they currently use would need to be completely restructured to preserve text messages. Our interviews with ATF and DEA also confirmed this.

FBI officials told ODAG it is now able to archive all text messages sent and received by its employees. FBI officials provided the OIG with an explanation regarding the technological limitations associated with archiving all text messages sent and received by its employees.

---

[61] A litigation hold (also known as preservation orders or hold orders) is a stipulation requiring a company to preserve all data that may relate to a legal action.

[62] The USMS was not a part of the working group. ODAG personnel stated that its absence from this meeting was an oversight.

Retention of Text Messages – FBI

An FBI Enterprise Security Operations Center (ESOC) official told the OIG that the FBI archives and proactively monitors the text messages of employees through the use of a proprietary database developed internally. Further, the FBI has disabled the ability to send images via employee BlackBerry devices. According to FBI officials responsible for managing this effort, the ESOC collects copies of BlackBerry diagnostic logs sent from Research in Motion (RIM), the company that makes BlackBerry devices.[63] The FBI preserves the diagnostic logs on the Criminal Justice Information Services (CJIS) servers for a period of 90 days. ESOC personnel told us they then store all the diagnostic logs they receive from RIM in a separate database at FBI headquarters for a period of 25 years. ESOC personnel can filter the data from these diagnostic logs based on a telephone number, a date, or the name of the recipient of the text message. The ESOC official said that keyword word searches are possible but can be more challenging.

ESOC officials also told us that generally the data obtained from these diagnostic logs is useful, but complained that data is often missing from the logs. According to the ESOC, there are several reasons for this. First, the diagnostic logs help debug functions and troubleshoot issues but do not comprise a complete audit history of text message content sent and

> **New Jersey Court Questions FBI's Text Message Preservation Capabilities**
>
> In *United States* v. *Suarez*, 2010 WL 4226524 (D.N.J. October 21, 2010), a key cooperating witness who assisted the government in its investigation of public corruption in New Jersey from 2008 through 2009 participated in multiple recorded meetings with targets of the investigation, during which the cooperator exchanged numerous text messages with three FBI agents. The exchange of text messages could be seen on video recordings and was visible to the defense when viewed. In response to a defense request, the FBI attempted to obtain the text messages but could not provide them all because they were erased in accordance with the FBI CJIS 90-day retention policy for storing BlackBerry diagnostic logs on their servers.
>
> Although the court found FBI had not acted in bad faith, it issued an adverse inference instruction allowing the jury to infer that the government's failure to preserve the text messages made this evidence relevant and favorable to the defendants. The jury acquitted the defendant whose defense counsel focused on the missing text messages, but convicted the other defendant, although a variety of factors may have contributed to this result.

---

[63] The FBI informed us that they are transitioning to Android phones. This switch may help address some of the issues with the FBI's current capabilities discussed below.

received and there is no requirement for their accuracy or completeness. In addition, we were told that the data contained in diagnostic logs is sometimes corrupted, resulting in the data being inaccessible. Further, ESOC officials told us they can only archive what they receive. If the FBI is not provided all data contained in the diagnostic logs, or if the data is corrupted, the FBI will not receive all the text messages sent and received by their employees.

Brady/Giglio Issues – FBI

These issues of lost data were brought to bear in *United States* v. *Suarez*, discussed in the text box. In that case, the FBI was asked for the first time to produce text message exchanges between a key cooperating witness and three FBI agents. The court found that the CJIS 90-day retention policy for storing BlackBerry diagnostic logs was the reason for the FBI's failure to produce the text messages.

ESOC officials told us that they were unable to produce the text message exchanges in the *Suarez* case because the FBI does not have control over the entire process of transmitting text message data sent on government issued devices. In fact, we learned that a large part of this process, for all the law enforcement components, is dependent on external phone and data networks. Before text message data is logged on CJIS servers, the data travels through cellular networks and the RIM network for BlackBerry devices. RIM will then forward text message data to CJIS, but we were told that in some cases the data may not arrive if there are encryption key issues or glitches in the external phone and data networks.[64] These weaknesses may continue to impact the FBI's ability to fulfill their discovery obligations.

Retention of Text Messages – USMS

We found that the USMS uses a process similar to the FBI process for archiving text messages. The USMS uses BlackBerry diagnostic logs to archive text messages, but it cannot detect the transmission of sexually explicit photographs or images.

However, there are two important differences. The USMS archives the text messages of its employees indefinitely. In addition, the USMS does not proactively monitor the transmission of sexually explicit text messages, even though we were told by the USMS that it has the ability to do so. Since USMS cannot detect sexually explicit photographs or images, we were unable to determine the actual number of "sexting" instances occurring at USMS during the study period.

---

[64] An encryption key is a sequence of numbers used to encrypt or decrypt data.

In interviews, USMS OPR-IA officials told us they have requested text messages for their investigations but could not easily obtain the evidence they need because it could not be filtered. The Inspectors said they would receive an entire day's text messages for all USMS employees and would have to sift through the records to determine what text messages related to their misconduct investigations. However, a USMS information technology Program Manager told us they can filter text messages and provided the OIG a detailed explanation on how this occurs. When we asked why they do not provide OPR-IA misconduct investigators with filtered text messages, the Program Manager stated that they do so on occasion, but generally misconduct investigators sort through the text messages themselves as some investigators are not aware of the filtering capability.

Since USMS can archive and filter the text messages sent and received by their employees, we find it troubling that its misconduct investigators are not fully aware of the filtering capability to identify specific text messages. OPR-IA officials commented to us that employees tend to speak freely via text message. One OPR-IA official stated, "If we were able to filter text message evidence for these [sexual misconduct] and all misconduct investigations, it would be of great benefit."

Brady/Giglio Issues – USMS

Even though USMS has the technology, USMS law enforcement witnesses are solely responsible for providing text messages that are potentially discoverable. By allowing USMS witnesses to independently make these determinations without further oversight or review, there is a risk these witnesses may not provide all relevant text messages or may adulterate the text messages before providing them. Further, since the USMS has the ability to archive the text messages of their employees, prosecutors should be given access upon request to the archived text messages especially in instances where suspected *Brady* or *Giglio* issues arise.

Retention of Text Messages – ATF

We were unable to determine the actual number of "sexting" cases occurring at ATF during the study period because ATF does not archive text messages sent and received by its employees. This means that potentially relevant information is not available for investigators conducting misconduct investigations.

In interviews with ATF officials, we learned ATF investigators often rely on text message evidence in misconduct investigations, particularly investigations where the conduct committed is sexual in nature or involved an alleged inappropriate relationship. However, investigators must request the evidence from the employees or retrieve their government-issued devices. We also learned that ATF does not proactively monitor the text messages of its employees. This inevitably hampers its ability to detect and deter misconduct by its employees, including sexual misconduct, on an ongoing basis.

ATF investigators told us that in most cases they must rely on the honesty of employees to provide all the relevant text messages sent and received. There are a number of risks to be considered when relying on such information, including that the employee supplying the information may not provide all the relevant material. In addition, the employee may adulterate the evidence by adding or removing language contained in the text message. The employee may also delete any incriminating text messages altogether before they can be retrieved through forensic imaging. We were told that once a text message is deleted in this manner it is nearly impossible to recapture it without obtaining a forensic image of the government-issued device, serving an administrative subpoena on the cellular network carrier, or obtaining a court order.[65]

Brady/Giglio Issues – ATF

Further, we were told that ATF law enforcement witnesses are solely responsible for providing text messages to prosecutors to satisfy discovery obligations under *Brady* and *Giglio*. By allowing ATF witnesses to independently make these determinations without further oversight or review, there is a risk that these witnesses may not provide all relevant text messages or may adulterate the text messages before providing them. Because there is no archive, prosecutors cannot independently obtain access to the text messages to address potential issues.

Retention of Text Messages – DEA

We found that, like ATF, DEA does not archive text messages sent and received by its employees. This similarly means that potentially relevant information may not be available for investigators conducting misconduct investigations and that DEA may be hampered in its ability to satisfy its discovery obligations. The ODAG also informed us that the DEA's current policy regarding the preservation of electronic communications for discovery purposes is not entirely consistent with the Deputy Attorney General's March 30, 2011, memo entitled *Guidance on the Use, Preservation, and Disclosure of Electronic Communications in*

---

[65] A forensic image is a forensically sound and complete copy of a hard drive or other digital media, generally intended for use as evidence. In addition, we were told that network carriers typically preserve the content contained in text messages for only 3 to 5 days, absent a Court order or other requirement for a longer preservation period.

Federal Criminal Cases, insofar as DEA does not require that all e-mail or text messages with outside witnesses be preserved.[66]

In interviews with DEA officials, we learned that the DEA would have to retrieve an employee's government-issued device in order to obtain text messages in connection with a misconduct investigation. And we were told that, if the employee deleted any text messages prior to the phone's retrieval, the DEA would be unable to recover them. DEA officials stated that the only other option available would be to issue an administrative subpoena or obtain a court order to receive the text message data directly from the cellular network carrier. The DEA officials we spoke with said they could not recall this ever occurring and, as discussed above, the information might well no longer be retained by the time such legal process was sought and obtained.[67]

We also learned that the DEA does not proactively monitor the text messages of its employees. As with the other components that do not do this, we believe that the DEA inevitably is hampered in its ability to detect and deter misconduct by its employees, including sexual misconduct, on an ongoing basis.

E-mail Preservation Issues Abroad – DEA

In interviews, we learned that the DEA experiences similar limitations when attempting to retrieve deleted e-mail messages from the 833 DEA employees stationed in foreign countries as of July 2013.[68] According to DEA officials, the DEA does not archive e-mails sent and received by employees stationed in foreign countries because the e-mails

---

[66] We were notified that the ODAG is currently working with the DEA to ensure consistent policies.

[67] During the OIG investigation involving allegations that DEA agents facilitated a sexual encounter for a supervisory Secret Service agent in Cartagena, Colombia, the DEA and the OIG had difficulties in retrieving text-message evidence from the DEA agents' BlackBerry devices because two of the agents deleted data from them prior to providing the devices to the OIG. DEA officials told us that forensic imaging proved impossible for one of the agents who had entirely "wiped" his device. Nevertheless, the investigation ultimately resulted in the DEA agents being charged with obstruction of an official investigation, among other charges. The DEA subsequently revoked the agents' eligibility for access to National Security Information (NSI). As of January 9, 2015, DEA's Chief Counsel Office stated that one of the DEA agents had appealed to the U.S. Court of Appeals for the Federal Circuit challenging his indefinite suspension without pay based upon the revocation of his security clearance.

[68] See DOJ OIG, *Review of Policies and Training Governing Off-Duty Conduct by Department Employees Working in Foreign Countries,* Report 15-2, January 2015.

do not go through DEA servers.[69] Officials in the DEA Office of Security Programs told us that a forensic image of the computer must be taken in order to retrieve deleted e-mails created on a DEA computer in use overseas.

Brady/Giglio Issues – DEA

Among the four law enforcement components, the DEA has the largest number of employees stationed overseas. We were told that many criminal prosecutions involving narcotics and prescription drug trafficking originate in or involve DEA overseas offices, raising additional concerns about whether these limits hamper the DEA's ability to satisfy its discovery obligations in these cases. Because there is no archive, even if the information is requested from the employees themselves, there is a risk that an employee may not provide all relevant material, may adulterate what is produced, or may simply delete the text and e-mail messages altogether. In the final section of this report, we discuss our conclusions and recommendations for improvement.

---

[69] If an e-mail is sent to a domestically located DEA employee, it would be archived as a received e-mail for that employee.

CONCLUSION AND RECOMMENDATIONS

Overall, we found there were relatively few reported allegations of sexual harassment and sexual misconduct in the Department's law enforcement components. However, while we had difficulties getting timely and complete information from the FBI and the DEA, even based on the information that we received our review of the handling of these allegations revealed some significant systemic problems with the disciplinary and security processes requiring corrective action across the four law enforcement components.

We determined that all the components have policies requiring some level of coordination between the offices responsible for ensuring employees meet the requirements to hold security clearances and the internal affairs offices who investigate misconduct allegations. At the FBI, all misconduct allegations are referred to the Security Division's Analysis and Investigation Unit to determine whether the allegation raises security concerns.

However, we found instances where ATF, DEA, and USMS employees engaged in a pattern of high-risk sexual behavior, but security personnel were not informed about these incidents until well after they occurred, or were never informed. By failing to refer these allegations to security personnel, the high-risk sexual behavior of these employees has the potential to expose ATF, DEA, and USMS employees to coercion, extortion, and blackmail and presents security risks for these components.

We were particularly troubled by multiple allegations involving several DEA special agents participating in "sex parties" with prostitutes while working in an overseas office. The misconduct occurred for several years while these special agents held Top Secret clearances. Many of these agents were alleged to have engaged in this high-risk sexual behavior while at their government-leased quarters, raising the possibility that DEA equipment and information also may have been compromised as a result of the agents' conduct.

Second, although ATF and the USMS have clear policies requiring supervisors to report to their headquarters internal affairs offices misconduct allegations, including alleged sexual misconduct and sexual harassment, we found instances in which supervisors failed to report these allegations, even when the alleged misconduct had occurred in the past.

At the DEA and the FBI, we found that policies on reporting allegations of misconduct provides supervisors with discretion when determining what to report and what to treat as a management or performance-related issue. We found an instance where supervisors at these components exercised that discretion even when their respective offense tables characterized the conduct as something that should be reported to headquarters.

Third, we determined that ATF, the DEA, and the FBI have criteria for determining whether to open an investigation at headquarters or refer it back to management in the field for handling. Although it appears that ATF consistently followed its criteria, at the FBI we found instances where it failed to open investigations at headquarters into allegations of serious sexual misconduct and sexual harassment when called for by its criteria. At the DEA, we found instances where the DEA OPR failed to fully investigate allegations of serious sexual misconduct and sexual harassment. The USMS has no criteria for making these determinations, but we found that it appropriately handled allegations in all the cases we examined.

Fourth, we determined that the DEA, FBI, and USMS offense tables contain specific offense categories to address allegations of sexual misconduct and sexual harassment and to provide guidance on the appropriate range of penalties that could be imposed. However, we found that these components often applied general offense categories to misconduct that fell within the more specific offense categories contained in their offense tables. In addition, we found that the ATF offense table does not contain specific offense categories to address sexual misconduct and sexual harassment.

While the FBI offense table contains specific language to address the solicitation of prostitutes overseas even where the conduct is legal, we found that ATF, the DEA, and the USMS offense tables do not contain specific language to address this form of misconduct. As a result of these issues, employees of the law enforcement components may not be fully notified as to the types of conduct that are prohibited, may not have adequate notice of the range of penalties that could be imposed, and there is also a risk that inconsistent penalties could be imposed for similar misconduct. Further, it may be difficult for the components to easily determine the frequency of this type of misconduct or to identify any trends in the types of allegations reported.

Fifth, we determined that all the law enforcement components do not have adequate technology to archive text messages sent and received by their employees and are unable to fully monitor the transmission of sexually explicit text messages and images. Therefore, we could not determine the actual number of instances involving the transmission of sexually explicit text messages, images, and e-mails, also known as "sexting." These same limitations limit the ability of the components to make this important information available to misconduct investigators and may risk hampering the ability of the components to satisfy their discovery obligations.

To correct the deficiencies discussed above, we make eight recommendations to improve the law enforcement components' disciplinary and security processes. We recommend that the Department and the law enforcement components develop consistent policies and practices to ensure that sexual misconduct and sexual harassment allegations are handled in an appropriate fashion and that information regarding such allegations is referred to security personnel for consideration in a timely manner. Specifically, we recommend:

1. All four law enforcement components should ensure that supervisors and managers report all allegations of sexual misconduct and sexual harassment to headquarters, and they should consider ensuring compliance with this requirement by including it in their performance standards so as to subject supervisors and managers to possible discipline for failing to report allegations.

2. ATF, DEA, and USMS should ensure that all non-frivolous sexual harassment and sexual misconduct allegations are referred to their respective security personnel to determine if the misconduct raises concerns about the employee's continued eligibility to hold a security clearance, and to determine whether the misconduct presents security risks for the component.

3. The components should have and follow clear and consistent criteria for determining whether an allegation should be investigated at headquarters or should be referred back to the originating office to be handled as a management matter.

4. All four law enforcement components should use the offense categories specifically designed to address sexual misconduct and sexual harassment, and revise their tables if they are inadequate or otherwise deter the use of such categories.

5. The Office of the Deputy Attorney General (ODAG) should ensure that the Department's zero tolerance policy on sexual harassment is enforced in the law enforcement components and that the components' tables of offenses and penalties are complimentary and consistent with respect to sexual harassment.

6. The Office of the Deputy Attorney General (ODAG) should develop policy explicitly prohibiting the solicitation of prostitutes in a foreign jurisdiction even if the conduct is legal or tolerated, and ensure that all component offense tables include language prohibiting this form of misconduct.

7. All four law enforcement components, in coordination with ODAG, should acquire and implement technology and establish procedures to effectively preserve text messages and images for a reasonable period of time, and components should make this information available to misconduct investigators and, as appropriate, for discovery purposes.

8. All four law enforcement components, in coordination with ODAG, should take concrete steps to acquire and implement technology to be able to, as appropriate in the circumstances, proactively monitor text message and image data for potential misconduct.

APPENDIX 1: METHODOLOGY

For this review, the OIG interviewed 72 officials at ATF, the DEA, the FBI, the USMS, the Office of the Deputy Attorney General, and the OIG's Investigations Division. We conducted a series of analyses to evaluate the nature and frequency of sexual harassment and sexual misconduct affecting the workplace and the security of operations. We evaluated the reporting, investigation, and adjudication phases. We considered whether supervisors failed to report allegations of sexual harassment and sexual misconduct. We also considered whether misconduct investigators opened investigations regarding the appropriate subjects and whether they focused on all the issues contained in the allegation. Further, we evaluated whether the law enforcement components offense tables are adequate to address sexual misconduct and sexual harassment allegations.

Data Collection

OIG requested case files and data points from each of the Department's four law enforcement components regarding all misconduct allegations arising during the period FY 2009 through and including FY 2012 (October 1, 2008, to September 30, 2012).[70] We included in this report misconduct allegations that were still open as of April 23, 2013, and updated the information during the course of our review.[71]

ATF

Prior to our formal initiation of this review, ATF provided us with data points for all of their misconduct cases and allowed the OIG to determine which cases fell within the scope of our review. We identified 94 allegations of a sexual nature and requested these case files. Upon reviewing the case files, we determined that 47 of the allegations were within the scope of our review. ATF provided unfettered access to this information and worked with the OIG to correct errors or fill in any missing data points.

---

[70] Component case files may contain multiple allegations against multiple subjects. For purposes of this review, we generally count each case file as a separate case and each subject of an investigation as a separate allegation. However, during adjudication, an adjudicative case file contains only information relating to an individual subject. Therefore, when discussing the adjudicative process, we refer to each subject as a case.

[71] Any open allegations of sexual misconduct or sexual harassment discussed in this report were monitored or investigated by the OIG.

<u>USMS</u>

The USMS also produced to us the information we requested prior to the formal initiation of this review. We reviewed 2,248 USMS misconduct allegations arising during the study period that were contained in a spreadsheet provided by the USMS. We determined that 98 potential allegations related to our review. After a more thorough review of the case files, we determined that 81 misconduct allegations were within the scope of our review. The USMS provided unfettered access to the case information and worked with the OIG to correct errors or fill in any missing data points.

<u>FBI</u>

Unlike ATF and the USMS, the FBI was initially unwilling to provide un-redacted information that we requested in April 2013 related to sexual misconduct and sexual harassment allegations arising during the study period. We elevated these issues for discussion and resolution with the respective component senior management. At the conclusion of the initial discussions, the FBI agreed to run a list of search terms the OIG developed to determine the allegations that related to sexual misconduct and sexual harassment.

In consultation with the OIG, the FBI developed a shorter list of terms that focused on seven offense categories relating to sexual misconduct and sexual harassment. Even after the OIG formally initiated this review in July 2013, the FBI provided substantially redacted information regarding 242 sexual misconduct and sexual harassment cases, as well as the data points related those cases. The FBI claimed that it could not provide the information to the OIG due to limitations in the *Privacy Act* and because the information contained Personally Identifiable Information (PII).[72] The OIG objected, advising the FBI that we were entitled to access the materials pursuant to Section 6 of the *Inspector General Act*. As we further informed the FBI, the prohibitions in the *Privacy Act* do not apply to the dissemination of materials by the Department to the OIG and the OIG handles all information that it receives consistent with the requirements in the *Privacy Act*. Additionally, the OIG regularly reviews PII in connection with its oversight responsibilities and, in this instance, our Investigations

---

[72] *See generally, Privacy Act of 1974*, Pub. L. 93–579, 88 Stat. 1896, 5 U.S.C. § 552a, which governs the collection, maintenance, use, and dissemination of personally identifiable information about individuals that is maintained in systems of records by federal agencies, and the Inspector General Act of 1978, § 6(a)(1) (authorizing OIGs "to have access to all records, reports, ... documents, papers, ... or other material available to the [agency] which relate to programs and operations with respect to which that Inspector General has responsibilities under this Act").

Division should have previously received these reports from the FBI at the time of the alleged event, pursuant to Department regulations requiring that Department components report non-frivolous allegations of misconduct to the OIG. We did not receive the un-redacted information we requested from the FBI until August 2013, some 4 months after our initial request.

We had the OIG Investigations Division search its case management system using our full list of search terms to try to help ensure that we had received all the cases within the scope of our review. Through this search, we identified a material number of additional allegations of sexual misconduct or sexual harassment that were not originally provided to us by the FBI. The discrepancy was greater than we could explain in light of the longer list of search terms used internally and the different databases searched.

Once we identified the discrepancies, we requested the information from the FBI. The FBI provided it to the OIG without substantial redactions and thereafter worked with the OIG to correct errors or fill in any missing data points. A further review of the information the FBI provided for these additional cases found that a material number of the cases contained the agreed upon search criteria. We were unable to determine why a material number of in scope cases were excluded from the FBI's production. The failure to provide case file information in a timely fashion unnecessarily delayed our work.

DEA

In April 2013, prior to our formal initiation of this review, we requested information related to sexual misconduct and sexual harassment allegations arising during the study period. Similarly to the FBI, the DEA initially was unwilling to provide the OIG with any of the information that we requested. Even after the OIG formally initiated this review in July 2013, the DEA provided only substantially redacted information regarding 67 sexual misconduct and sexual harassment cases, as well as the data points related to those cases. As with the FBI, the DEA cited the *Privacy Act* and concerns for the individuals involved as the basis for not providing the information. We provided a lengthy list of sexual misconduct-related search terms to the DEA and requested that it use the terms to search its database for sexual misconduct cases. We did not receive un-redacted information in response to this request until September 2013, some 5 months after our initial request and only after we informed the DEA that the FBI had produced similar material to us in August 2013. Further, after a working draft of our report was issued to the components, the DEA informed us that it did not run our full list of search terms but instead ran only three search terms in conjunction with a search by offense code.

As with the FBI, we had the OIG Investigations Division search its case management system to ensure the information finally produced to us by the DEA was complete and responsive to our request. We identified a material number of additional allegations of sexual misconduct or sexual harassment that were not originally provided to us by the DEA. We requested this information from the DEA and it was provided to us, although the DEA continued to redact some of the information.

Based upon our analysis of the DEA's search process, we determined that a significant number of cases were within the scope of our review and met even the DEA-selected search criteria but were not provided to the OIG during their initial un-redacted production. Moreover, even after DEA agreed to provide the additional case files, it continued to redact some of the information. The failure to provide case file information in a timely fashion unnecessarily delayed our work.

Cleaning and Normalizing the Misconduct Data

Charges applied to misconduct allegations are general and may not adequately describe the conduct to allow for comparisons, for example, *Conduct Unbecoming a Federal Employee.* After identifying the allegations relating to sexual misconduct and sexual harassment, we standardized the offense categories and created a data field containing standardized offense categories or types. This allowed us to better characterize the misconduct and to make comparisons across the law enforcement components and among demographic categories, such as position, race, and grade level.

In addition, we created data fields to better categorize the allegations, such as identifying the allegations in which an allegation was not substantiated, the law enforcement component chose not to discipline an employee, or the outcome was not clear based on documentation in the case file. We then completed descriptive statistical analysis of the misconduct case data.

Analysis of Referrals

To determine whether matters were reported to the OIG, we reviewed each component's initial complaint for a notation that the allegation was referred. We identified only two allegations where this notation was not present but confirmed the allegations were in fact referred with the OIG Investigations Division.

Interviews

We interviewed 72 officials at ATF, the DEA, the FBI, the USMS, the Office of the Deputy Attorney General, and the OIG's Investigations

Division who were involved in the reporting, investigation, and adjudication phases of the disciplinary process. We also interviewed misconduct investigators and proposing/deciding officials regarding specific sexual harassment and sexual misconduct allegations. In addition, we interviewed information technology professionals at the respective components who are responsible for archiving employee e-mails and text messages. Further, we interviewed representatives from each component's Office of General Counsel regarding discovery issues. When necessary, we conducted additional interviews to resolve any follow-up questions and confirm our findings.

We also were concerned by an apparent decision by DEA to withhold information regarding a particular open case. The OIG was not given access to case file information until several months after our initial request. Once we became aware of the open-case information, DEA employees we interviewed about it stated that they were given the impression that they were not to talk to the OIG about this case while it remained open. We were able to re-interview the officials; but the OIG was entitled to receive all such information from the outset and the failure to provide it unnecessarily delayed our work.

Case File Review

We reviewed case files related to sexual misconduct. The case files included documentation such as the initial complaint form, the interview transcripts, the summary of investigative findings, the proposal letter, and the decision letter. We first evaluated whether the allegations fell within the scope of this review. We also evaluated whether misconduct investigators opened investigations regarding the appropriate subjects and whether they focused on all the issues contained in the allegation. Further, we evaluated whether an allegation was an area of concern pursuant to the Adjudicative Guidelines, and whether the allegation was reported to the appropriate security personnel.

When reviewing the case files, we identified allegations that were not handled appropriately in at least one phase of the disciplinary process. We created a "Problem Case" data field and marked cases accordingly. We then conducted analysis on this metric. During our case file review, we identified cases where supervisors failed to report alleged sexual harassment and sexual misconduct and where internal affairs offices failed to open misconduct investigations when doing so was warranted. We also identified cases in which an investigation was opened, but the investigation lacked obvious due diligence such as failing to interview alleged witnesses or failing to investigate additional subjects that came to light during the course of the investigation.

Data Analysis

We identified allegations that it appeared were not handled appropriately in at least one phase of the disciplinary process, including reporting, investigation, and security issues. We created a data field to mark these cases and analyzed the frequency of these issues. We conducted an overall demographic analysis of the subjects, to include race, gender, and grade level, but did not identify any trends or patterns.

In addition, we conducted a timeliness analysis of each component's disciplinary process. We divided the allegations into two categories, formal discipline and informal discipline. For the allegations that resulted in informal discipline, we also included allegations that were administratively closed with no action taken. This allowed us to compare timeliness across components for allegations that went through the entire disciplinary process (those ending in formal discipline) as well as the cases that went through only a part of the disciplinary process (those ending in informal discipline/administrative closure).[73]

Policy Review

We reviewed each component's policies, procedures, and guidance related to sexual harassment and sexual misconduct. These reviews enabled us to identify deficiencies in these policies and their implementation. These policy reviews also informed the interviews we conducted, the case file reviews, and our data analysis.

---

[73] We conducted an analysis of the length of time it took the law enforcement components to investigate and adjudicate sexual misconduct and sexual harassment allegations. Because many of the cases (e.g., child pornography, sexual abuse, and the solicitation of prostitutes domestically) went through the criminal process or were investigated by the OIG, the data was skewed significantly. Therefore, our analysis did not show a true reflection of the length of time it took the law enforcement components to handle these types of allegations.

APPENDIX 2: LAW ENFORCEMENT COMPONENT DISCIPLINARY PROCESSES

The description of each component's disciplinary process is based on the OIG's review of the written policies and procedures related to the respective component disciplinary process and interviews with component officials and staff members responsible for the investigation and adjudication of discipline and adverse actions.

The Bureau of Alcohol, Tobacco, Firearms and Explosives (ATF)

The mission of ATF is to conduct criminal investigations, regulate the firearms and explosives industries, and assist other law enforcement agencies. In 2013, ATF had 4,719 employees, of which 2,402 served as Special Agents, 791 served as Industry Operations Investigators, and 1,526 served in other positions. In addition, currently, 4,657 ATF employees hold a security clearance level of Secret or higher.

ATF Disciplinary Process

ATF supervisors are required to report all allegations of misconduct to the Internal Affairs Division (IAD).

Four entities are involved in the ATF disciplinary process: (1) the Internal Affairs Division (IAD); (2) the Office of Professional Responsibility, Security Operations (OPRSO); (3) the Professional Review Board (PRB); and (4) the Bureau Deciding Official (BDO).

Reporting Allegations of Sexual Misconduct and Harassment[74]

ATF Order 8610.1B requires allegations to be reported to the IAD. A duty agent documents the allegation and any relevant evidence in an incident report. To determine whether an allegation should be investigated on a preliminary basis, should be designated as a headquarters internal investigation, or should be referred back to the reporting field division "for action" or "information only," the incident report is reviewed by the Assistant Special Agent in Charge (ASAC) and the Special Agent in Charge (SAC) of the Internal Affairs Division. The Assistant Director (AD), Office of Professional Responsibility and Security Operations (OPRSO) make the final decision on the type of investigation initiated.

---

[74] *See generally* ATF Order 8610.1B, *Integrity and Other Investigations,* March 9, 2012.

In addition, the IAD reports to the OPRSO, Security and Emergency Programs Division (SEPD), Personnel Security Branch (PSB), conditions that could raise a security concern. Depending upon the seriousness of the allegation, the PSB may suspend an employee's eligibility for access to classified information pending the conclusion of the IAD investigation.

Investigating Allegations of Sexual Misconduct and Harassment[75]

Most allegations concerning employee integrity, ethical, or criminal violations are designated as internal investigations from their inception. Where additional facts must be gathered to determine the nature and seriousness of the misconduct, a preliminary investigation is conducted at headquarters, but it may be converted into an internal investigation if the nature of the allegation so warrants. All preliminary investigations must be completed in 45 days.

If the allegation involves a minor infraction of ATF policy or is performance related, it may be referred back to the field division as a management referral. There are two types of management referrals, "For Action" or "Information Only." Management referrals "For Action" require the field divisions to conduct an inquiry and report their findings to the IAD within 60 days of their receipt.

When the field division management concludes the inquiry, they consult the Chief Counsel's Administrative and Ethics Division to determine if discipline is warranted. Where an incident report is drafted, but the allegation lacks specificity or does not involve an ATF employee, the IAD may refer the matter back to the field division as a management referral for "Information Only." These referrals do not require further inquiry or consultation with the IAD or the ATF Chief Counsel.

During an internal investigation, ATF investigators collect evidence and signed, sworn statements and conduct interviews. At the conclusion of an internal investigation, the investigator prepares the final report of investigation containing a statement of the facts. No conclusions or statements of substantiation are contained in the final report. The IAD has approximately 120 days from receipt of the allegation to complete an internal investigation and refer the final report to the Professional Review Board. The AD OPRSO reviews and approves all reports of investigation before they are sent to the Chair of the ATF Professional Review Board.

---

[75] ATF Order 8610.1B, *Integrity and Other Investigations,* March 9, 2012.

Adjudicating Reports of Investigation[76]

The Professional Review Board consists of five members who meet monthly to review reports of investigation received from Internal Affairs Division or the DOJ OIG. ATF defines non-adverse actions as letters of reprimand and suspensions of 14 days or less. An adverse action constitutes a suspension of 15 days or more, removal, demotion, reduction in pay, or a furlough for 30 days or less.

If the Board determines that there is sufficient evidence of misconduct warranting disciplinary action, the Board consults case precedent and the ATF Table of Offenses and Penalties to determine the appropriate penalty. In some cases, disciplinary action may not be warranted and a letter of clearance is issued to the subject employee. Where disciplinary action is warranted, a Human Resources Specialist drafts a proposal letter containing the recommended discipline. The Professional Review Board's goal is to issue proposal letters within 30 days of the Board's receipt of the report of investigation.

The Bureau Deciding Official renders discipline decisions based on the report of investigation, the Board's proposal, and the employee's response.[77] The report of investigation supporting the proposed disciplinary action is usually attached to the proposal letter, and the employee is permitted to hire a representative in preparation. Once the Deciding Official receives the employee's response, the BDO considers the relevant Douglas Factors, and has a goal to render a decision within 30 days.[78] The Deciding Official can reduce the penalty proposed by the Board but may not increase it.

After the final decision letter is issued, the employee's management must ensure the proscribed penalty is imposed. For a suspension of 14 days or less, an employee may seek review of the BDO's decision by

---

[76] ATF Order 2140.1, *Adverse Action and Discipline,* November 29, 2011, and ATF Order 2141.2, *Professional Review Board,* September 5, 2006.

[77] For a suspension of 14 days or less, 5 C.F.R. Part 752 § 203 requires the components to provide the employee with a reasonable amount of time, but not less than 24 hours, to make an oral or written reply to the proposal letter. Where the penalty is a suspension of 15 days or more, removal, demotion, furlough, or a reduction in pay, the employee has at least 7 days to make an oral or written response. *See* 5 U.S.C. Chapter 75 and 56 C.F.R. Part 752 § 203 and 404.

[78] Under civil service laws, there are 12 factors, known as the Douglas Factors, which should be considered in determining the appropriateness of a disciplinary penalty. See *Douglas* v. *Veterans Administration,* 5 M.S.P.B. *313 (1981). See* Appendix 5 for a list of the 12 Douglas Factors.

filing a grievance with the official designated in the decision. An employee may appeal a suspension of 15 days, including a removal before the Merit Systems Protection Board (MSPB).[79]

ATF Guide for Offenses and Penalties[80]

The ATF *Guide for Offenses and Penalties* does not contain specific offense categories designed to address allegations of sexual misconduct, but it describes conduct equivalent to sexual harassment or inappropriate behavior of a sexual nature within the offense categories *Inappropriate Behavior* and *Poor Judgment and/or Conduct Unbecoming a Federal Employee/Special Agent.* For sexual harassment, the ATF Guide contains an offense category directed at supervisors for failing to report allegations of sexual harassment, but it does not define sexual harassment. The explanations in the ATF Guide also contain a number of general offense categories under which sexual misconduct could be charged.

The Drug Enforcement Administration

The mission of the DEA is to enforce the controlled substances laws and regulations of the United States. In 2013, the DEA had 11,053 employees, of which 5,250 served as Special Agents and 5,803 served in other support capacities. In addition, currently, 9,401 DEA employees hold clearances at the Secret level or higher.

DEA Disciplinary Process

There are three entities involved in the DEA disciplinary process: (1) the Office of Professional Responsibility (OPR); (2) the Board of Professional Conduct (HRB); and (3) the DEA Deciding Officials.[81]

---

[79] The Merit Systems Protection Board (MSPB) is an independent, quasi-judicial agency in the Executive Branch that hears appeals of various agency decisions, most of which are appeals of agencies' adverse actions in discipline cases.

[80] ATF *Guide for Offenses and Penalties*, March 9, 2010.

[81] The DEA OPR investigates Task Force Officers (TFO) in the same manner as permanent employees. However, the adjudication of TFOs by the DEA is handled by their division management. ATF, the FBI, and the USMS do not investigate misconduct allegations involving TFOs unless the incident involves one of their permanent employees.

Reporting Allegations of Sexual Misconduct and Sexual Harassment[82]

Once an allegation is reported to the OPR, the allegation must be given a designation or code before it is assigned for investigation. There are three possible designations made by the Deputy Chief Inspector (DCI) or the Associate Deputy Chief Inspector (ADCI) based on how specific the allegations are at the time of reporting. The designation also indicates whether the Inspector assigned is permitted to obtain signed, sworn statements from the subject and other witnesses. The three designations are Administrative (AD), Professional Responsibility (PR), and Information Gathering Field (IGF). Each designation is discussed in more detail in the next section.

Investigating Allegations of Sexual Misconduct and Sexual Harassment

An allegation is designated as an Administrative (AD) where there is not sufficient evidence at the time of reporting to determine if a possible integrity violation occurred. AD inquiries must be completed within 30 days of the receipt of the allegation. The Inspector assigned to an AD case is not permitted to elicit signed, sworn statements. If an AD preliminary inquiry develops sufficient evidence to determine that a possible integrity violation occurred, an AD case may be converted to either an IGF or a PR case.

An allegation is designated as a Professional Responsibility (PR where there is a clear indication of an integrity violation. PR cases involve criminal activity and violations of the DEA Standards of Conduct. Employees are typically charged under the general offense category *Failure to Follow Instructions* or *Poor Judgment* when they commit an integrity violation. PR investigations must be completed in 180 days or less. Only PR cases are forwarded to HRB and Deciding Officials for disciplinary action.

An allegation is designated as Information Gathering Field (IGF) where the initial allegation is vague and requires the Inspector assigned to gather additional information. IGF cases typically include loss of property or fiscal offenses and are charged under the general offense category *Conduct Unbecoming a DEA Agent or Non-Agent.* The Inspector assigned to PR and IGF cases may elicit signed, sworn statements from subjects and witnesses. If an IGF case develops to the point that a particular DEA employee violated the Standards of Conduct, it is converted to a PR case so that it can be forwarded to the HRB and the Deciding Officials.

---

[82] DEA *Office of Professional Responsibility* Handbook, undated.

Further, an IGF case can be converted to a PR case once additional information is obtained. IGF investigations must be completed in 90 days or less. However, if an IGF-designated allegation is converted to a PR investigation, the PR investigation time standard of 180 days is applied from the date of conversion. Once a designation is made and the case is assigned, a DEA OPR Inspector initiates a preliminary inquiry to determine whether the allegation should be fully investigated, referred back to field division management for handling (management referral), or administratively closed.

During the preliminary inquiry and throughout the investigation process, the DEA OPR Inspector also evaluates whether the allegation raises security concerns for the DEA or whether the allegation compromises the employee's continued ability to hold a security clearance. When security issues are present, the assigned Inspector consults the ADCI or the DCI, who have the sole discretion to determine whether the allegation warrants referral to the Office of Security Programs (OSP). If a referral is made, the DEA OPR provides investigative support.

If there is no indication of misconduct, or that a DEA employee or Task Force Officer (TFO) was involved, the matter is administratively closed. If an allegation is referred back to the field, field management may also be required to conduct further inquiries and report what they learn to the DEA OPR. If a full investigation is warranted, the Inspector gathers additional evidence and interviews witnesses. When the investigation is completed, the assigned Inspector prepares a final report containing a statement of facts learned. No conclusions or statements of substantiation are contained in the final report. Before the final report is sent to the Chair of the Board of Professional Conduct, it must be approved by the ADCI or DCI.

Adjudicating Reports of Investigation[83]

The Chair of the Board of Professional Conduct assigns cases to one of the three Board members. Unlike the ATF Professional Review Board, the DEA HRB is not a Board with voting members. Instead, the Board is staffed with three proposing officials who review the report of investigation, case precedent, and the DEA Guide of Disciplinary Offenses and Penalties to determine the appropriate penalty.

Like ATF, Human Resources Specialists draft the proposal letter before it receives a final review by the Chair. For letter of reprimands and suspensions of 14 days or less, there is no Chief Counsel review

---

[83] DEA *Human Resources Manual on Discipline*, March 17, 2005.

before the proposal letter is sent to the DEA Deciding Officials. Where the proposed penalty is a suspension of 15 days or more up to removal, the DEA Chief Counsel's Office must review the proposal letter for legal sufficiency.

Once this proposal letter is issued, the employee has an opportunity to provide an oral or written response, or both, to the Deciding Officials assigned to their case.[84] DEA employees may also seek representation. Unlike the other components, DEA employees are not provided a copy of the final report of investigation. Instead, they may review the report in DEA space to prepare their response and take notes. When rendering a decision, the DEA Deciding Officials also consider the report of investigation, the proposal letter, case precedent, the relevant Douglas Factors, and any oral or written response.

After the final decision letter is issued, the employee's management must ensure the prescribed penalty is imposed. For suspension of 14 days or less, an employee may grieve the decision with the official designated in the decision letter. For suspensions of 15 days or more up to removal, an employee may appeal the decision before the MSPB.

DEA Guide for Disciplinary Offenses and Penalties[85]

The DEA *Guide of Disciplinary Offenses and Penalties* contains seven offense categories that could presumably address allegations of sexual misconduct and sexual harassment, including *Unprofessional or Inappropriate Conduct of a Sexual Nature, Sexual Harassment,* and *Retaliation against an Employee Resulting from or in Connection with an Allegation of Sexual Harassment.* However, the only penalty suggested for *Sexual Harassment* is removal. Other offense categories that do not specifically address sexual misconduct but may, under certain circumstances, be considered sexual misconduct are *Improper Association with a Convicted Felon, Confidential Source and/or Persons Connected with Criminal Activity; Disrespectful or Unprofessional Conduct;* and *Criminal, Dishonest, Infamous or Notoriously Disgraceful Misconduct.* These categories provide a range of penalties that can be applied.

The Federal Bureau of Investigation

The mission of the FBI is to protect and defend the United States against terrorist and foreign intelligence threats; to uphold and enforce the criminal laws of the United States; and to provide leadership and criminal justice services to federal, state, municipal, and international

---

[84] 5 U.S.C. Chapter 75 and 56 C.F.R. Part 752 § 203 and 404.

[85] DEA *Guide for Disciplinary Offenses and Penalties,* undated.

agencies and partners. In 2013, the FBI had 35,344 employees, of which 13,598 served as Special Agents and 21,746 served as Intelligence Analysts, Language Specialists, Scientists, Information Technology Specialists, and in other support capacities. Further, all FBI staff hold clearances at the Top Secret level or higher.

FBI Disciplinary Process[86]

There are four entities involved in the FBI disciplinary process: (1) the Internal Investigations Section (IIS), Inspection Division (INSD); (2) the Office of Professional Responsibility (OPR) Proposing Officials and Deciding Officials; (3) the Human Resources Division (HRD); and (4) the Disciplinary Review Board (DRB).

Reporting Allegations of Sexual Misconduct and Sexual Harassment[87]

The Internal Investigations Section (IIS) is the unit of the Inspection Division responsible for overseeing the initial processing and investigation of misconduct allegations. All allegations of employee misconduct must be in writing before the Initial Processing Unit (IPU) enters the allegation into the case management system. If the allegation is not specific, or cannot be attributed to a specific FBI employee, the assigned Conduct Review Specialist may request additional information from the field. In addition, the FBI IIS refers all allegations of misconduct to the Security Division (SecD), Analysis and Investigations Unit (AIU) for a determination as to whether the allegation raises security risks for the FBI or whether the allegation raises concerns about the employee's ability to hold a security clearance. If these risks are present, the AIU opens a parallel investigation.

Investigating Allegations of Sexual Misconduct and Sexual Harassment

The Lead Conduct Review Specialist, IPU Unit Chief, and the Section Chief review the allegation to determine whether to open an investigation at headquarters, delegate the investigation to the field with IIS oversight, or administratively close the matter. Allegations are generally closed where there is insufficient evidence to warrant an investigation. When making these determinations, the reviewers rely on

---

[86] The procedural protection afforded to most employees in the federal service does not apply to most FBI employees. For example, FBI employees cannot appeal disciplinary decisions to the Merit Systems Protection Board like most other federal employees (5 U.S.C. § 7511(b)(8)). In addition, FBI policy does not require the proposing officials and deciding officials to be walled off from one another when adjudicating discipline.

[87] FBI *Internal Investigations Section IIS, Supervisors' Guide*, Version 6, March 2013.

their experience and the FBI Offense Codes and Penalty Guidelines. It is within the sole discretion of the IIS Section Chief to open or close an allegation.

If an investigation is opened at headquarters, or in the field with IIS oversight, a Supervisory Special Agent (SSA) or Assistant Inspector in Place (AIIP) collects all evidence and signed, sworn statements and conducts interviews. At the conclusion of the investigation, the investigation case file is forwarded to the FBI Office of Professional Responsibility for adjudication.

Adjudicating Reports of Investigation[88]

The Office of Professional Responsibility (OPR) adjudicates all allegations of misconduct involving FBI employees. The OPR reviews all relevant facts and evidence, case precedent, and the Douglas Factors when preparing a report. If the allegation is substantiated, the FBI OPR determines the proposed penalty and final decision.

For oral reprimands, letters of censure, and suspensions of 14 days or less (non-adverse actions), there is no formal proposal stage in the process and one of the two Adjudication Unit Chiefs determines the discipline imposed. For suspensions of 15 days or more, including removals (adverse actions), the Unit Chiefs propose discipline and the Assistant Director makes the final decision. However, the Assistant Director must approve all proposal letters. When rendering the final decision, the Assistant Director considers the employee's oral and/or written reply to the allegations. The Assistant Director may not impose a penalty greater than the proposal. Generally, the FBI attempts to complete the investigation and adjudication of a misconduct case within 180 days.

Although most of the procedural protections outlined in the Code of Federal Regulations do not apply to FBI employees, a non-probationary FBI employee may appeal non-adverse actions to the Human Resources Division (HRD). Non-disciplinary counseling, oral reprimands, and letters of censure are not appealable. The Disciplinary Review Board, which is chaired by the Assistant Director and is made up of five FBI employees, both agents and non-agents, decide appeals of adverse actions (suspensions of 15 days or more up to removal).

---

[88] The Office of Professional Responsibility (OPR), which is part of the Director's Office, is headed by an Assistant Director who reports directly to the Deputy Director. OPR has two adjudication units, each of which is headed by a Unit Chief. *See* generally, FBI *Policy Implementation Guide for Adjudication of Delegated Disciplinary Matters*, Office of Professional Responsibility, March 2013.

FBI Offense Codes and Penalty Guidelines[89]

The FBI *Offense Table and Penalty Guidelines* contains six offense categories that specifically address sexual misconduct allegations. The FBI table provides guidance on the range of discipline for sexual misconduct – consensual as described above and provides guidance on the types of penalties resulting from engaging in improper relationships. These offenses include improper relationships with a criminal element; with a subordinate/superior; and with an asset, confidential witness, or informant.

The table further provides guidance on penalties where an employee engages in indecent/lascivious acts and sexual harassment with a broad range of penalties.

The United States Marshals Service

The mission of the USMS is to enforce federal laws and provide support to virtually all elements of the federal justice system. In 2013, USMS had 5,602 employees, of which 94 served as U.S. Marshals, 3,925 as Deputy U.S. Marshals and Criminal Investigators, and 1,583 as Detention Enforcement Officers and administrative employees. In addition, 3,063 USMS employees currently hold clearance levels at the Secret level or higher.

USMS Disciplinary Process

There are three entities involved in the USMS disciplinary process: (1) the Office of Professional Responsibility, Internal Affairs (OPR-IA); (2) the USMS Proposing Officials; and (3) the USMS Deciding Official.

Reporting Allegations of Sexual Misconduct and Sexual Harassment[90]

The USMS employs a three-tier evaluation process to determine whether an allegation of misconduct warrants full investigation, should be referred back to the originating office (district or division) as a management referral, or discretionarily closed due to insufficient evidence. When an allegation of misconduct is reported to USMS Internal Affairs, the Deputy Chief Inspector, the Chief Inspector, and the Deputy Assistant Director review the allegation at the outset to make these determinations. If there is insufficient evidence, reviewers discretionarily close the matter.

---

[89] FBI *Offense Codes and Penalty Guidelines,* January 15, 2012.

[90] *USMS* Policy Directive, 2.2. *General Operations, Critical Reporting Requirements,* undated.

Investigating Allegations of Sexual Misconduct and Sexual Harassment[91]

Where there is sufficient evidence, but the reviewers believe the misconduct warrants a suspension of 14 days or less (discipline), OPR-IA refers the matter back to the originating office for investigation. The OPR-IA reviewers rely on their institutional knowledge, but do not consult the USMS Table Disciplinary Offenses and Penalties when determining if an allegation warrants full investigation or referral back to the originating office.

In addition, if the allegation raises security concerns for USMS or affects the employee's continued ability to hold a security clearance, and the allegation is fully investigated at headquarters, the OPR-IA Chief Inspector refers the matter to the Office of Security Programs, Tactical Operations Division (OSP TOD). OSP TOD does not receive information about matters referred back to the originating office.

If the matter warrants full investigation, USMS Inspectors collect evidence and signed sworn statements and conduct interviews. At the conclusion of the investigation, the Inspector writes a final report of investigation. USMS has a goal to complete a headquarters investigation within 90 days. At the close of the investigation, the final report is sent to the USMS Proposing Officials for adjudication.

Adjudicating Reports of Investigation[92]

The USMS has two adjudication processes depending upon the severity of the proposed action to be taken based on the results of the investigation conducted.

Letters of Reprimand and Suspensions of 14 Days or Less (Discipline)[93]

Once an allegation is referred back to the field, district or division management work with the Discipline Management Unit (DM) to collect additional evidence, complete an incident or field report, and, ultimately, impose discipline. Typically, DM Human Resources Specialists consult the offense tables, determine case precedent, and obtain the Douglas Factors from the field to draft the proposal and decision letters. In some cases, the originating office drafts the letters with Discipline

---

[91] *USMS* Policy Directive, 2.2, *General Operations, Critical Reporting Requirements,* undated.

[92] USMS *Policy Directive, Human Resources,* 3.3, *Performance & Related Matters, Discipline and Adverse Actions,* 2007.

[93] Unlike the other components, the USMS issues a formal proposal and decision letter where the proposed penalty is a letter of reprimand.

Management's assistance. DM has a goal to complete the adjudication of a management referral within 120 days.

For these cases, the Chief Deputy U.S. Marshal or division counterpart serves as the proposing official in discipline cases, while the U.S. Marshal or Division counterpart serves as the Deciding Official. Employees subject to discipline may make an oral or written response, or both, to their respective Deciding Officials, and may grieve the decision to the official designated in the decision letter.

Suspensions of 15 days or More up to Removal (Adverse Actions)

For suspensions of 15 days or more up to removal, the two USMS Proposing Officials are responsible for proposing disciplinary action, while the USMS Deciding Official renders discipline decisions. The USMS Proposing Officials are assigned cases based on their availability. When drafting the proposal, the Proposing Official consults the final report of investigation, case precedent, and the offense tables to determine the appropriate penalty.

Unlike some of the other components that use Human Resources Specialists to draft the proposal letter, the USMS Proposing Officials draft the proposal letters for adverse actions cases. The USMS Office of General Counsel also reviews for legal sufficiency all letters where adverse action is proposed. Once the proposal letter is approved by General Counsel, it is issued to the employee and their district or division management.

To maintain the independence of the USMS Proposing and Deciding Officials, the Discipline Management Unit (DM) provides the USMS Deciding Official with the final report of investigation and the proposal letter to render a decision. Like the other components, USMS employees are provided a reasonable period of time (10 days) to make an oral and/or written reply to the USMS Deciding Official.

The USMS Deciding Official reviews the final report of investigation, case precedent, the employee oral and/or written reply, and the Douglas Factors when rendering a discipline decision. The Office of General Counsel also reviews the decision letter for legal sufficiency. Once approved, the final decision letter is issued and the employee is advised that they may appeal the decision before the MSPB. If there is no appeal, district or division management must ensure the proscribed penalty is imposed.

USMS Guidance Table of Disciplinary Offenses and Penalties[94]

The USMS *Guidance Table of Disciplinary Offenses and Penalties* is virtually identical to the DEA *Guide for Disciplinary Offenses and Penalties* and contains six offense categories that could presumably address allegations of sexual misconduct, including *Unprofessional or Inappropriate Conduct of a Sexual Nature, Sexual Harassment,* and *Retaliation against an Employee Resulting from or in Connection with an Allegation of Sexual Harassment.*

Other offense categories that do not specifically address sexual misconduct, but may under certain circumstances be a type of sexual misconduct, are *Improper Association with a Convicted Felon, Confidential Source and/or Persons Connected with Criminal Activity,* and *Disrespectful or Unprofessional Conduct.*

Standards of Conduct

All of the components have specific policies, often referred to as their standards of conduct, which inform employees of the behavior expected of them. After reviewing the standards of conduct of the law enforcement components, we learned that they offer specific guidance related to sexual harassment and inappropriate relationships, but not other forms of sexual misconduct. Generally, the components' offense tables provide more information.[95]

---

[94] USMS *Guidance Table of Disciplinary Offenses and Penalties,* May 3, 2012.

[95] *See generally* ATF Order 2130 1A, *Conduct and Accountability,* February 7, 2012; DEA *Personnel Manual,* Section 2735.15(A)(1), *Standards of Conduct,* undated; USMS Policy Directives, *Code of Professional Responsibility,* January 8, 2009; FBI *Ethics and Integrity Program Policy Implementation Guide* 0454PG, October 5, 2011; and the FBI *Personal Relationships Policy,* March 27, 2001. For more information about the law enforcement components' standards of conduct, refer to the OIG Evaluation and Inspections Report, 15-2, January 2015, *Review of Policies and Training Governing Off-Duty Conduct by Department Employees Working in Foreign Countries.*

APPENDIX 3: LAW ENFORCEMENT COMPONENT OFFENSE TABLES – SEXUAL MISCONDUCT AND SEXUAL HARASSMENT

Law Enforcement Offense Tables – Sexual Misconduct and Sexual Harassment

ATF Offenses	Explanation
Association with Disreputable Persons	Includes, but not limited to, improper personal relationships with convicted felons, informants, and subjects of investigations. **Admonishment to Removal**
Conduct Prejudicial to the Government	Includes criminal, infamous, dishonest, immoral, or notoriously disgraceful conduct, or other conduct prejudicial to the government. **Removal**
Failure by Supervisor to Report Allegations of Sexual Harassment	No explanation provided. **Admonishment to Removal**
Inappropriate Behavior	Includes, but not limited to, inappropriate actions directed toward co-workers, subordinates, or supervisors. Also includes behavior (e.g., teasing, jokes, gestures, display of materials) of a sexual, sexual orientation, gender nature. Also includes intimidating, threatening, sexually insensitive remarks. **Admonishment to Removal**
Poor Judgment and/or Conduct Unbecoming a Federal Employee/ Special Agent	Includes, but not limited to, conviction of a criminal offense, engaging in sexual activity in ATF office space, and creating an embarrassing situation for the Bureau. **Admonishment to Removal**

DEA Offenses	Explanation
Conduct Unbecoming a DEA Employee	No explanation provided. **Reprimand to Removal**
Criminal, Dishonest, Infamous, or Notoriously Disgraceful Misconduct	No explanation provided. **14-Day Suspension to Removal**
Disrespectful or Unprofessional Conduct	Includes use of insulting, abusive, or obscene language, angry outbursts, disrespectful comments, provoking quarrels, or inappropriate remarks. **Reprimand to Removal**
Improper Association with a Convicted Felon, Confidential Source and/or Persons Connected with Criminal Activity	All DEA employees are held accountable for this type of behavior. **Reprimand to Removal**

DEA Offenses	Explanation
Retaliation against an Employee Resulting from or in Connection with an Allegation of Sexual Harassment	Any person who has been found to have engaged in the act of retaliation. **Reprimand to Removal**
Sexual Harassment	As defined in Title VII of the *Civil Rights Act of 1964* **Removal**
Unprofessional or Inappropriate Conduct of a Sexual Nature	Includes teasing, jokes, actions, gestures, display of materials, or remarks of a sexual nature. **Reprimand to Removal**

FBI Offenses	Explanation
Asset/CW/Informant/CHS (Source) – Improper Personal Relationship	Engaging in a social, romantic, or intimate relationship or association with a source. **Letter of Censure to Removal**
Disruptive Behavior	Engaging in inappropriate verbal or physical conduct while on official business. Disruptive Behavior or in an FBI space or vehicle, which is disruptive or negatively impacts the workplace. **Oral Reprimand to 10 Days**
Improper Relationship – Criminal Element	Without authorization, engaging in an ongoing social, romantic, or intimate relationship or association with a person involved in criminal activities. **Letter of Censure to Removal**
Improper Relationship with a Subordinate	Engaging in or seeking a romantic or intimate relationship with a subordinate that violates the strictures of the FBI's Personal Relationships Policy. **Letter of Censure to Removal**
Indecent/Lascivious Acts	Inappropriately acting in a manner to appeal to or gratify the sexual desires of the employee, his victim, or both or indecently exposing a body part to public view. **5-Day Suspension to Dismissal**
Other Felonies	Engaging in an act which is considered a felony in the jurisdiction in which the act occurred. **10-Day Suspension to Removal**
Other Misdemeanors	Engaging in an act which is considered a misdemeanor in the jurisdiction in which the act occurred. **Letter of Censure to Removal**
Sexual Harassment	Making unwelcome or unwanted sexual advances, requesting sexual favors, or engaging in other verbal or physical conduct of a sexual nature. **Letter of Censure to Removal**

FBI Offenses	Explanation
Sexual Misconduct – Consensual	Engaging in sexual, intimate, or romantic activity with a willing partner(s) in an inappropriate location or while on duty. **Letter of Censure to Removal**
Unprofessional Conduct – Off Duty	Engaging in conduct, while off duty, which dishonors, disgraces, or discredits the FBI; seriously calls into question the judgment or character of the employee; or compromises the standing of the employee among his peers or his community. **Oral Reprimand to Removal**
Unprofessional Conduct – On Duty	Engaging in conduct, while on duty, which dishonors, disgraces, or discredits the FBI; seriously calls into question the judgment or character of the employee; or compromises the standing of the employee among his peers or his community. **Letter of Censure to Removal**

[1] Prior to January 2012, this offense category was previously known as "Sexual Misconduct – Non-Consensual." When a revision of the FBI offense table occurred, the category name was changed to "Sexual Harassment." There is no material difference in the explanations provided for both offense categories.

USMS Offenses	Explanation
Conduct Unbecoming a USMS Employee	No explanation provided. **Reprimand to Removal**
Conduct Which Creates a Reasonable Belief that the Employee Has Committed a Crime for Which a Sentence of Imprisonment May Be Imposed	No explanation provided. **Indefinite Suspension to Removal**
Conviction of a Law Enforcement Officer of a Felony	No explanation provided. **Removal**
Criminal, Dishonest, Infamous, or Notoriously Disgraceful Misconduct	No explanation provided. **14-Day Suspension to Removal**
Disrespectful or Unprofessional Conduct	Includes disrespectful comments and inappropriate remarks. **Reprimand to Removal**
Improper Association with a Convicted Felon, Witness Protection Program Participant, Confidential Source and/or Persons Connected with Criminal Activity	All USMS employees are held accountable for this type of behavior. **Reprimand to Removal**

USMS Offenses	Explanation
Retaliation against an Employee Resulting from or in Connection with an Allegation of Sexual Harassment	Any person who has been found to have engaged in the act of retaliation. **5-Day Suspension to Removal**
Sexual Harassment	As defined in Title VII of the *Civil Rights Act of 1964,* as amended. **5-Day Suspension to Removal**
Unprofessional or Inappropriate Conduct of a Sexual Nature	Includes teasing, jokes, actions, gestures, display of materials, or remarks of a sexual nature. **Reprimand to Removal**
Violations of the Code of Professional Responsibility	No explanation provided. **Reprimand to 14-Day Suspension**

Sources: Component offense tables.

APPENDIX 4: SEXUAL MISCONDUCT AND SEXUAL HARASSMENT OFFENSE CATEGORY ANALYSIS

The law enforcement components often applied general offense categories, for example, *Conduct Unbecoming a Federal Employee,* to various types of allegations of sexual misconduct and sexual harassment. To conduct the offense category analysis, we reviewed the misconduct case files to determine the nature of the sexual misconduct and sexual harassment that occurred in each case. We created standardized offense categories to allow us to better characterize the misconduct and to make comparisons across the components and among demographic categories such as position, race, and grade level.[96]

After normalizing the offense categories, we analyzed the frequency with which sexual misconduct or sexual harassment was alleged to have occurred in each component. We assessed the rate that this type of alleged misconduct occurred by population and determined the types of alleged offenses that occurred most often.

Rate of Sexual Harassment and Sexual Misconduct Allegations by Population

Based on the number of reported alleged offenses involving sexual harassment and sexual misconduct, the FBI had the lowest rate of this type of misconduct. The USMS had the highest rate of this type of misconduct. Table 2 describes the rate of sexual misconduct and harassment by population.

Table 2: Rate of Sexual Harassment and Sexual Misconduct Allegations by Population

	Employees	Total Offenses	Rate by Population
ATF	4,719	51	10.8
DEA	11,053	136	12.3
FBI	35,344	343	9.7
USMS	5,602	91	16.2

Sources: Component misconduct case files and annual reports.

---

[96] For the purposes of this analysis, we isolated all the sexual misconduct and sexual harassment offenses. Many subjects were alleged to have committed additional offenses that were not sexual in nature (for example, "Lack of Candor"). Therefore, we removed those offenses from our analysis.

ATF has 4,719 employees. There were 51 alleged sexual misconduct and sexual harassment offenses. For every 1,000 ATF employees, there were 10.8 alleged offenses of this type.

The DEA has 11,053 employees. There were 136 alleged sexual misconduct and sexual harassment offenses. For every 1,000 DEA employees, there were 12.3 alleged offenses of this type.

The FBI has 35,344 employees. There were 343 alleged sexual misconduct and sexual harassment offenses. For every 1,000 FBI employees, there were 9.7 alleged offenses of this type.

The USMS has 5,602 employees. There were 91 alleged sexual misconduct and sexual harassment offenses. For every 1,000 USMS employees, there were 16.2 alleged offenses of this type.

We also looked at the types of sexual misconduct and sexual harassment allegations that were reported at each law enforcement component. Table 3 shows the number of alleged sexual misconduct and harassment allegations by offense type.

Table 3: Alleged Sexual Misconduct and Sexual Harassment by Offense Type

Offense Categories	ATF	DEA	FBI	USMS	Total
Inappropriate Relationship (Supervisor/Subordinate and Colleagues)	10	18	77	15	120
Sexting	14	23	36	13	86
Sexual Harassment	3	28	50	4	85
Misuse of Government Property to Facilitate Sexual Activity (Office/Vehicle)	4	8	56	6	74
Inappropriate Sexual Comments and/or Gestures	9	1	29	22	61
Improper Association with a Criminal Element	3	13	9	8	33
Solicitation of Prostitutes (Overseas)	0	19	6	1	26
Solicitation of Prostitutes (Domestic)	1	2	15	1	19
Supervisor Failure to Report Sexual Misconduct	2	2	8	4	16
Alleged Sexual Assault	0	3	10	3	16
Alleged Sexual Abuse (Minor)	1	3	11	1	16
Improper Association with a Confidential Source	1	7	6	0	14
Child Pornography	1	2	7	1	11
Retaliation for Reporting Sexual Misconduct/Harassment	0	1	9	0	10
Obstruction of an Official Investigation	0	3	5	1	9
Alleged Sexual Abuse (Inmate)	0	0	0	8	8
Indecent Exposure	0	0	3	3	6
Videotaping Undressed Women without Consent	0	1	3	0	4

Offense Categories	ATF	DEA	FBI	USMS	Total
Assault	0	2	0	0	2
Solicitation of Sex (Multiple Partners)	1	0	1	0	2
Inappropriate Relationships (Foreign Nationals)	0	0	1	0	1
Misuse of Position (Strip Club)	0	0	1	0	1
Unprofessional Conduct – Off Duty (Strip Club)	1	0	0	0	1
Grand Total	51	136	343	91	621

Sources: Component misconduct case files.

Inappropriate Relationship (Supervisor/Subordinate and Colleagues)

Across the law enforcement components, the offense category analysis showed there were 120 total alleged offenses involving "Inappropriate Relationship (Supervisor/Subordinate and Colleagues)." Nineteen percent of the total number of alleged sexual misconduct and sexual harassment offenses involved this offense category.

As compared to the other components, "Inappropriate Relationship (Supervisor/Subordinate and Colleagues)" was alleged to have been committed more often than any other offense at the FBI. At the FBI, there were 77 alleged offenses of this type, or 22 percent of the total number of sexual harassment and sexual misconduct offenses.

Sexting

The second most common alleged offense was the transmission of sexually explicit texts, e-mail messages, or images, known colloquially as "sexting." We were unable to fully analyze this offense category because the law enforcement components do not have the technology to detect the transmission of sexually explicit images or photographs sent via text message. Therefore, we only analyzed the alleged offenses reported to their respective internal affairs offices.

The offense category analysis showed that there were 86 total alleged offenses involving sexting. Fourteen percent of the total number of alleged sexual misconduct and sexual harassment offenses involved this offense category.

As compared to the other components, sexting was alleged to have been committed most often at ATF. There were 14 alleged offenses of this type, or 27 percent of the total number of alleged offenses.

Sexual Harassment

The third most common alleged offense involved behavior we considered sexual harassment. The offense category analysis showed there were 85 total alleged offenses of this type. Fourteen percent of the total number of alleged sexual misconduct and sexual harassment offenses involved this offense category.

The DEA and the FBI had the majority of alleged offenses involving sexual harassment. At the DEA, there were 28 alleged offenses of this type and 50 alleged offenses at the FBI.

Solicitation of Prostitutes (Overseas)

There were 26 total allegations involving the "solicitation of prostitutes (overseas)." These allegations constituted 4 percent of the total number of alleged sexual misconduct and sexual harassment offenses.

The DEA had the majority of alleged offenses involving "solicitation of prostitutes (overseas)." There were 19 alleged offenses of this type, or 14 percent of the total number of alleged offenses.

APPENDIX 5: DOUGLAS FACTORS

The Merit Systems Protection Board, in its landmark decision, *Douglas* v. *Veterans Administration,* 5 M.S.P.R. 280 (1981), established criteria that supervisors must consider in determining an appropriate penalty to impose for an act of employee misconduct.

Although not an all-inclusive list, the following factors must be considered, when relevant, in determining the severity of the discipline:

1. The nature and seriousness of the offense, and its relation to the employee's duties, position, and responsibilities, including whether the offense was intentional or technical or inadvertent, or was committed maliciously or for gain, or was frequently repeated;

2. The employee's job level and type of employment, including supervisory or fiduciary role, contacts with the public, and prominence of the position;

3. The employee's past disciplinary record;

4. The employee's past work record, including length of service, performance on the job, ability to get along with fellow workers, and dependability;

5. The effect of the offense upon the employee's ability to perform at a satisfactory level and its effect upon supervisors' confidence in the employee's work ability to perform assigned duties;

6. The consistency of the penalty with those imposed upon other employees for the same or similar offenses;

7. The consistency of the penalty with any applicable agency table of penalties;

8. The notoriety of the offense or its impact upon the reputation of the agency;

9. The clarity with which the employee was on notice of any rules that were violated in committing the offense, or had been warned about the conduct in question;

10. The potential for the employee's rehabilitation;

11. Mitigating circumstances surrounding the offense such as unusual job tensions, personality problems, mental impairment, harassment, or bad faith, malice or provocation on the part of others involved in the matter; and

12. The adequacy and effectiveness of alternative sanctions to deter such conduct in the future by the employee or others.